SHELBY STATE LIBRARIES

Teen Crime Wave
A Growing Problem

Jeffrey A. Margolis

—Issues in Focus—

Enslow Publishers, Inc.
44 Fadem Road PO Box 38
Box 699 Aldershot
Springfield, NJ 07081 Hants GU12 6BP
USA UK

This book is dedicated to my wife, Ida, for her support and encouragement in the development of this book.

Copyright © 1997 by Jeffrey A. Margolis

All rights reserved.

No part of this book may be reproduced by any means without the written permission of the publisher.

Library of Congress Cataloging-in-Publication Data

Margolis, Jeffrey A.
   Teen crime wave: a growing problem / Jeffrey A. Margolis.
     p. cm. — (Issues in focus)
   Includes bibliographical references and index.
   ISBN 0-89490-910-X
   1. Juvenile delinquents—United States—Juvenile literature.
2. Juvenile delinquency—United States—Prevention—Juvenile literature. 3. Juvenile homicide—United States—Juvenile literature. 4. Juvenile justice, Administration of—United States—Juvenile literature. I. Title. II. Series: Issues in focus (Hillside, N.J.)
HV9104.M265 1997
364.36'0973—dc21   96-53650
                                                                          CIP
                                                                              AC

Printed in the United States of America

10 9 8 7 6 5 4 3 2 1

Illustration Credits: Steven Bamberg, pp. 33, 58, 75; The Historical Society of Pennsylvania, pp. 8, 19, 22, 70; Library of Congress, p. 42; Ida Margolis, p. 26; Jeffrey A. Margolis, pp. 47, 82, 90; Snyder, Howard N., and Sickmund, Melissa. (1995). *Juvenile Offenders and Victims: A National Report.* Washington, D.C.: Office of Juvenile Justice and Delinquency Prevention, pp. 13, 73, 96; Superior Court of New Jersey, County of Cape May, p. 65.

Cover Illustration: Eric R. Berndt/Photo Network

Contents

	Acknowledgments	. . . .	4
1	The Exploding Crisis	. . . .	5
2	The History of Juvenile Justice in America	. . . .	16
3	What Causes Juvenile Crime?	. . .	29
4	How the Juvenile Justice System Works	. . . . .	40
5	Juvenile Crime: A View From Two Cities	. . . .	55
6	The Debate: Should Juveniles Be Tried as Adults?	. . .	67
7	New and Innovative Programs	. . .	78
8	The Future	. . . .	94
	Chapter Notes	. . . .	99
	Glossary	. . . .	105
	Further Reading	. . . .	106
	Index	. . . .	111

Acknowledgments

This book could not have become a reality without the efforts of the faculty and students of the Richard M. Teitelman School in Cape May, New Jersey. I also wish to thank Detective Michael Brogan and the Lower Township, New Jersey, Police Department for their cooperation.

1

The Exploding Crisis

Appleton, Wisconsin, is a typical large American city of sixty-five thousand. Typical, too, in the sense that it had a gang problem; one that led to a gruesome murder-suicide. On May 2, 1995, three members of a gang known as D-Mac Crew lured seventeen-year-old Jermaine Gray, a member of a rival gang called the Gangster Disciples, into a cottage about one hundred miles from Appleton. Gray had been harassing gang members and owed them a $250 drug debt. The D-Mac Crew members murdered Gray by first choking him, then stabbing him, and finally bashing his head with a rock. About a week later, in an effort to destroy the victim's body, gang members moved it from one site to another, poured gasoline over it, and then set it on fire. Three members of the gang, one sixteen years of age and one seventeen, were arrested in connection with the killing. Three other gang members involved in the murder plot, one sixteen-year-old and two eighteen-year-olds, killed themselves with a .25 caliber handgun.

Juvenile Crime Rising

The above story is a grim one, but it is only one example of juvenile crime in this country, which is reaching alarming proportions. Recent crime data released by the Federal Bureau of Investigation (FBI) and other agencies show a large increase in the number of juveniles arrested for violent crimes. According to the FBI, the number of juveniles arrested for homicide between 1983 and 1992 increased 128 percent, as opposed to the 9 percent increase among the adult population.[1]

> A 1991 U.S. Centers for Disease Control (CDC) survey showed that one in twenty students in grades nine through twelve carries a firearm at least once a month. According to the CDC, in 1986, firearm homicide became the second leading cause of death among 15 to 19 year olds.[2]

Statistics point to the fact that juvenile crime has become a major American crisis not only for the police and the courts, but for doctors and hospitals as well. In 1992 the Surgeon General of the United States, Antonia C. Novello, said that deaths from gunfire had become a public health crisis. The *Journal of the American Medical Association* stated that gunshot wounds were a leading cause of death among high school age children.[3]

Are these facts surprising given the knowledge that the United States has the highest murder rate in the industrialized world? While some figures indicate that the crime rate in America is going down, the number of violent crimes such as murder, rape, and assault are, in fact, on the rise. In 1992, for example, law enforcement agencies made over 2 million arrests of persons under the age of eighteen. Of those arrests, 3,330 were for murder, 45,700 were for robbery, 74,400 were for aggravated assault, and 85,700 were for drug offenses.[4] In all, crimes committed by juveniles made up 13 percent of all violent crimes reported to law enforcement agencies and 18 percent of all violent-crime arrests in 1992. The states with the highest arrest rates were New York, Florida, New Jersey, Maryland, and California.[5]

Violence in Schools

Even schools, which for a long time had been considered safe places for young people, have been the scene of increased violence. On February 26, 1992, the mayor of New York City, David Dinkins, was scheduled to speak to the students at Thomas Jefferson High School in Brooklyn. Because this school had a history of violence, extra police and security guards were sent to the school to patrol the building before the mayor's speech. Not long before Dinkins's arrival, there was a shooting in the hallway. Two teenage boys were shot—both of them died.[6]

School is the place that many people are counting on to help solve the juvenile crime problem. Teachers and counselors who care about young people are trying to educate them to prepare them for jobs so they will not have to turn to crime for money. School is also the place where young people are taught about the dangers of drugs and alcohol. In schools, young people learn how to

Juvenile crime is not unique to the late twentieth century—it was a serious concern in the United States more than one hundred years ago. This nineteenth-century Sunday school newspaper illustration depicts young boys, on the left, stealing a girl's piece of candy. The illustration served as a warning that such acts could lead to a life of crime and eventual residence in a prison cell.

resolve problems without fighting. Yet schools have often become violent and dangerous places.

The stories of school violence are in our newspapers and on television every day. In March 1993, a high school student in Harlem, Georgia, opened fire in a school hallway, killing one student and wounding another. In November 1992, an elementary school principal was shot and killed on the street outside his school while looking for a missing student. In September of that same year, six students were shot in Amarillo, Texas, when a seventeen-year-old started shooting in the hallway after a pep rally.

Philadelphia has been dealing with the major problem of violence in its public schools. In 1994, according to school records, more than one thousand weapons were taken from students. Thirty-five of those weapons were guns. Over one thousand students, five hundred teachers, and two hundred fifty other workers were assaulted in Philadelphia's public schools. Every day, special school-district police deal with many of these violent acts. These include assaults, bomb scares, thefts, drug charges, and vandalism.[7] Lieutenant Daniel Placentra of the Philadelphia Police Department is in charge of a program that makes surprise visits to city high schools with portable metal detectors to randomly search students on their way into school.

The Martin Luther King High School is just one of the city's problem schools. During the 1993-94 school year there were over 357 serious incidents. This led to 171 arrests, the highest number in any city school. More and more violent acts are being reported and are handled by the school police instead of the principal.

School violence is not just limited to big cities. A few years ago, in a junior high school in southern New Jersey, four eighth-grade students, three boys and a girl, placed rat poison in a teacher's coffee cup. Although the teacher was not seriously injured, the four students were arrested, required to appear in juvenile court, and expelled from school for the remainder of the year. Incidents in which both students and teachers are injured or killed have become more commonplace. According to the U.S. Secretary of Education, approximately 3 million thefts and violent crimes take place on or around school grounds every year. One in every five high school students regularly carries either a knife, gun, razor, or some other weapon to school.

Many schools today require students to wear picture ID cards to school in an effort to keep out unwanted intruders. School districts may even have metal detectors that students must pass through every morning. Some school districts have employed armed police officers specially trained and assigned to the schools on a full-time basis. Other districts bring drug-sniffing dogs into school buildings to check student lockers. In Long Beach, California, one junior high school built a ten-foot-high, three-hundred-foot-long concrete wall around the school for protection against drive-by shootings and random bullets.

Students have reported being beaten and robbed of their sneakers or their jewelry. Others have been attacked for wearing the colors of a rival gang. Still other students have been assaulted for their religious beliefs or cultural backgrounds, or because they were gay or lesbian.

Incidents of school violence such as the one at Sullivan High School in the Midwest have become all too frequent. Sullivan is a school with about fourteen hundred students. In November 1993, a gang argument broke out across the street from the school at about noon. Kati Faber, a fifteen-year-old freshman, was shot at the scene. She died at a hospital about an hour and a half after the incident. The shooter was a sixteen-year-old boy who used a .380 semiautomatic handgun. The gun had been held for him in school by his girlfriend. While the case against the boy is still pending, the girl was convicted of murder in juvenile court under an Illinois law. This law states that an accessory to a murder—one who helps out—is also accountable for that crime.[8]

The spread of juvenile violence has not been limited to schools and teenagers. In what might be considered one of the youngest acts of violence, a six-year-old girl in Modesto, California, stabbed a seven-year-old in the back. The fight was about Barbie dolls. The six-year-old went to her apartment and returned with a steak knife, threatening to kill the other girl. The seven-year-old was treated in the hospital for a two-and-a-half-inch-deep wound in her back. Police Lieutenant Tim Atchley said that there was little the police or courts could do because of the girl's age. She was released and turned over to her parents. Atchley said, "Our society is becoming more and more violent every day."

The outlook for the future does not seem much better. One reason is the expected changes in the age range of our population. Since the mid-1980s, juvenile violence has grown faster than the juvenile population; murder arrests of youths under eighteen, for example, have more than doubled.

As federal government reports have shown, juveniles have become the victims of crimes as well as the perpetrators. Robert "Yummy" Sandifer, an eleven-year-old boy from Chicago, is a sad example.

A Short and Violent Life

On August 28, 1994, Yummy (Robert's friends called him that because of his love for cookies and candy) was involved in a gang shoot-out. Using a 9mm semiautomatic handgun, he shot and killed a fourteen-year-old girl named Shavon Dean. Three days later, Yummy was found shot to death with two bullets in the back of his head. His body was left under a railroad bridge on the South Side of Chicago. He, too, was the victim of gang violence.

Yummy had a long police record for such a young boy. In his short and violent life he was charged with twenty-three felonies and five misdemeanors. The charges included robbery and auto theft. He bullied other neighborhood children for money and was often absent from school. He also set cars on fire. Police and juvenile court judges did not know what to do with Yummy. He was placed in detention centers but ran away. Because he was so young, many of the juvenile group homes in the area refused to take him. Sandifer had a reputation for acting on impulse and was often unpredictable. He joined the notorious "Black

Juvenile Arrest Rates
(Arrests per 100,000 juveniles ages 10–17)

State	% Reporting	Violent Crime Index	Murder	Forcible Rape	Robbery	Agg. Assault
Total U.S.	83	458	12	22	161	263
Alabama	93	220	11	9	61	139
Alaska	94	205	1	23	38	143
Arizona	94	519	11	16	114	378
Arkansas	100	265	14	22	60	168
California	99	633	20	17	246	350
Colorado	92	506	6	21	85	394
Connecticut	82	499	7	24	125	343
Delaware	54	340	3	54	62	220
Dist. of Columbia	100	1,318	65	52	416	785
Florida	92	739	12	29	247	450
Georgia	72	251	6	14	62	169
Hawaii	100	276	2	26	149	99
Idaho	88	313	2	9	16	287
Illinois	42	463	5	52	101	305
Indiana	51	487	4	11	60	411
Iowa	64	159	0	9	17	133
Kansas	77	377	4	11	77	285
Kentucky	96	331	5	12	64	250
Louisiana	60	569	23	26	129	391
Maine	82	128	2	19	28	80
Maryland	100	645	21	35	200	390
Mass.	66	545	5	19	137	384
Michigan	90	388	20	44	101	223
Minnesota	99	179	3	12	29	136
Mississippi	35	223	15	31	73	105
Missouri	43	571	18	23	154	376
Montana	90	94	1	16	19	58
Nebraska	73	104	1	13	32	59
Nevada	79	394	25	39	145	185
New Hamp.	81	101	0	15	25	61
New Jersey	97	691	7	30	253	402
New Mexico	56	382	4	15	55	308
New York	85	996	15	17	642	322
N. Carolina	97	396	14	13	72	298
N. Dakota	77	58	0	15	13	30
Ohio	66	372	7	41	155	168
Oklahoma	97	353	8	24	90	231
Oregon	95	338	5	27	130	177
Pennsylvania	84	463	9	26	185	243
Rhode Island	100	613	4	33	82	494
S. Carolina	96	200	6	20	28	147
S. Dakota	71	120	2	23	8	87
Tennessee	49	296	12	23	100	161
Texas	100	380	17	17	131	214
Utah	73	391	2	26	56	307
Vermont	53	36	3	9	3	21
Virginia	100	228	11	20	92	105
Washington	80	385	5	48	106	226
West Virginia	100	77	3	9	24	41
Wisconsin	98	376	16	21	149	190
Wyoming	95	82	2	10	5	65

Source: State rates were developed from data reported in *Crime in the United States 1992*.

In recent years, the states of New York, Florida, New Jersey, Maryland, and California had the highest juvenile violent crime arrest rates.

Disciples," a gang with widespread membership in Chicago. He was on the run from police who were looking to question him about the murder of Shavon when he was killed.

Prior to his death, home life for Yummy was desolate and dangerous. He never knew his father and was beaten and abused by his mother, a cocaine addict who also had a long arrest record. Sandifer was sent to live with his grandmother, who was not able to control him either. Even though he was supposed to be living with her at the time, he was not. Sandifer was trying to contact her at the time of his murder.[9]

The story of Robert Sandifer is another example of the tragic rise in juvenile crime that is sweeping the United States. According to a 1991 survey, juveniles were responsible for 19 percent of all violent crimes reported to the National Crime Victimization Survey. The survey also stated that "17% of all serious violent crimes (in 1991) were committed by juveniles either acting alone or in groups. An additional 8% of serious violent crimes were committed by a group of offenders that included at least one juvenile and one adult."[10] In the United States, more than twenty thousand people die each year from violent acts, while another 2.2 million are injured. Incredibly, more than ten thousand young people between the ages of ten and twenty-four are murdered or commit suicide each year. Over half of the people arrested for murder in the United States in 1991 were under the age of twenty-five.[11]

The purpose of this book is to explore the issue of juvenile crime in America as well as the laws and policies of our juvenile justice system. In the following chapters we will look at the history of juvenile crime in America and how it has been dealt with. We shall also examine how the laws protecting young people have changed. Finally we shall examine some of the programs that schools and communities are using to help reduce the threat of juvenile crime and to try to rehabilitate young people who have committed crimes.

2

The History of Juvenile Justice in America

One of the earliest incidents of violent juvenile crime to be reported occurred in 1786.

One day during the summer of that year, twelve-year-old Hannah Ocuish, who was retarded, lured six-year-old Eunice Bollis to a secluded area outside of a town in Connecticut. She knocked her down and killed her. Hannah tried to hide the body but it was discovered the next day. Hannah was accused of committing the crime.

Hannah's attorney told her to plead not guilty. Despite the fact that Hannah was young and of low intelligence, she was found guilty of the murder. On October 12, 1786, Hannah was sentenced to the death penalty. She was hanged ten weeks later.[1]

Early History of Juvenile Justice

The laws governing the treatment of juveniles go back to colonial times. Many of these laws in the colonies were based on English law and laws of the church. Children under the age of seven could not be held guilty of serious crimes. "Between the ages of 8-14, their legal status was ambiguous. . . . Anyone over the age of 14 was presumably judged as an adult, although some colonies made exceptions."[2] In 1650, the Connecticut Code was written, outlining twelve major crimes. These included murder, rape, theft, and witchcraft. Even though most juveniles received lesser punishments than adults for these crimes, there was a record of a case where a twelve-year-old girl from the Pequot Indian tribe was hanged for killing a six-year-old white girl. There was another case, one year later, where a fourteen-year-old slave boy was branded and whipped one hundred lashes for helping in the murder of his master.

Before 1800, the behavior of children was the primary responsibility of the parents, particularly the father. The community and the church took a harsh view of those parents who could not or would not control their children. There were, however, many juveniles who ended up before judges in colonial times. The judges did not know what to do with the youths. They sent them to jail for a short time, but they often returned to court shortly after their release. There were even gangs. A newspaper story, appearing in Philadelphia in 1791, discussed the problem of juvenile gangs in that city.

The idea of treating juveniles differently from adult criminals did not come about until the 1800s. One of the first formal institutions dealing with "juvenile delinquency" was the House of Refuge. These houses were similar in many ways to the reform schools in England.

Established in 1825, in New York City, under the supervision of the newly formed Society for the Reformation of Juvenile Delinquents, the purpose of the House of Refuge was to "house juveniles convicted of criminal offenses or found in vagrancy."[3] This is the first instance in which the community decided to take some responsibility for young people whose parents were not able to control them. Within the next three years, additional houses were opened in Boston and Philadelphia.

Residents of the House of Refuge followed a very strict lifestyle. They were required to attend class, pray every day, and work as apprentices for local merchants and craftsmen. If they broke any of the house rules, they could be whipped. In 1849, a separate House of Refuge for Colored Juvenile Delinquents was opened in Philadelphia, and later, others were opened in New York and Boston. Additional separate facilities were established for girls. From this very early stage, the notion of discrimination became apparent. This was the beginning of separate treatment for minorities in our legal system. The issue of discrimination still persists today; minority juveniles make up a large percentage of the young people who are imprisoned.

In the mid-1800s, many state and local governments began to look for ways to control juvenile delinquents. As a result, they began to build "reform schools." These schools emphasized not only formal educational subjects but military-style drilling, physical fitness training, and vocational skills education as part of their total programs. Some of these schools eventually changed their names to "industrial schools" or "training schools."[4] Some of these

The Philadelphia House of Refuge as it appeared in 1835.

programs were not very different from the "boot camp" programs that we have today, which will be discussed in Chapter 7.

Between 1850 and 1890, a group of reformers called the "Child Savers" developed several ideas to help prevent juvenile delinquency. The groups tried to reform young people and prevent them from becoming serious criminals. Centers were opened to distribute food and clothing and to provide temporary shelter for children who were homeless. These Child Savers believed that the Houses of Refuge did not help enough young people. They believed, like the earlier generations of Americans, that keeping families together was the best way to prevent the continued rise in juvenile crime.

The best-known example of these groups was the Children's Aid Society. One of their plans was to take orphaned and adandoned city children and place them with farm families in the midwestern United States.[5] There were many documented cases of urban children ending up on farms. The purpose of this program was both to teach the youths about the work ethic and to provide them with a clean and safe place to live.

A very important event relating to the welfare of juveniles was the creation and establishment of the first juvenile court in the United States. In 1899, the Illinois legislature passed a law establishing courts that specifically dealt with children under the age of seventeen. These courts would hear cases dealing with delinquent as well as neglected children. In addition, the courts were given the responsibility of dealing with truancy and lack of parental supervision. As a result of these court proceedings, young offenders could be placed on probation, in foster homes, or in orphanages.[6]

The federal government did not take any real interest in the juvenile crime problem until the twentieth century. As a result of the White House Conference on Youth held in 1909, the United States Children's Bureau was established. This office evolved into an organization that provided guidelines for the treatment of abused, neglected, and delinquent youths.[7]

In the post-World War II era, signs began to point to a rapid rise in juvenile crime in this country. During the past forty years, several federal laws were passed to help deal with the juvenile crime problems. In 1951, a Juvenile Delinquency Bureau was created as part of the Department of Health, Education and Welfare. This was the result of the previously enacted Youth Corrections Act.

A Youth Offenses Act was passed by Congress in 1961 but lasted for only six years. During that time the government spent approximately $47 billion to deal with juvenile crime, but the program was not successful.

Seven years later, in 1968, the federal government tried to deal with the growing juvenile crime rate again by enacting the Juvenile Delinquency and Prevention Act. The purpose of this law was to provide money to deal with the various parts of the youth crime problem in our country. But even these efforts were not successful in slowing or stopping juvenile crime growth.

As the juvenile crime rate grew in America, the federal government continued to look for ways to deal with this rising epidemic. Then, in 1974, Congress enacted

The young residents of a House of Refuge were closely supervised.

the Juvenile Justice and Delinquency Prevention Act, an important set of laws. They were "designed specifically to prevent young people from entering the juvenile justice system and to assist communities in developing more sensible and economic approaches for youngsters already in the juvenile justice system."[8] One major change did occur. The Office of Juvenile Justice and Delinquency Prevention was to be controlled by the Department of Justice, not the Department of Health and Human Services.

"The Juvenile Justice and Delinquency Prevention Act was the first legislation to not only authorize federal funds but even to acknowledge any federal responsibility for the delinquency problem."[9] This act has been changed several times since 1974.

Juvenile crime is still a major concern today, and it is expected to continue to be a problem in the future. According to an article in *U.S. News and World Report*,

> since the mid-1980's, juvenile violence has grown faster than the juvenile population; murder arrests of youths under 18 have more than doubled. . . . Violence is committed disproportionately by young men and soon there will be more young men in the United States than at any time in history.[10]

One college professor said that "the fear of juvenile crime has come to affect how we view young people, where we go and at what time of the day, what businesses we patronize, and even our voting habits."[11]

The more recent history of the juvenile justice system in this country can be linked to several important decisions of the United States Supreme Court. In concluding this chapter we will review several of their key decisions that changed the way our legal system dealt with juveniles.

United States Supreme Court Decisions

United States Supreme Court decisions have had a major effect on the juvenile justice laws in our country. There have been several important cases that dealt with juveniles and their constitutional rights. Two are especially important: *Kent v. United States* and In re *Gault*.

Kent *v.* United States. Morris Kent first appeared in juvenile court in Washington, D.C., when he was fourteen years old. He was charged and judged as a delinquent for attempted purse snatching and for breaking into several houses. As a result, Kent was placed on probation. Probation is a key part of the juvenile justice system. In an effort to help young people who have gotten in trouble with the law, the juvenile court judge assigns a counselor or mentor who offers guidance and tries to help the juvenile stay out of trouble. These men and women are called probation officers. Their other responsibility is to report back to the juvenile court judge from time to time to inform the court about the progress of the juvenile.

Two years later on September 2, 1961, when Morris Kent was sixteen, he broke into an apartment in Washington, D.C., raped a woman who lived there, and stole her wallet. When he appeared in juvenile court, the judge decided to have Morris tried as an adult in a criminal court. This is called waiving juvenile court jurisdiction. This decision was very significant for Morris Kent. If his case had remained in juvenile court, the maximum sentence would have been for Morris to be sent to a reform school until he was twenty-one years old. However, by going to criminal court, Morris Kent could have been sentenced to death or to life imprisonment.[12]

Kent was indicted on all charges and convicted of the housebreaking. He was found not guilty of the other charges by reason of insanity. Kent was sentenced to a term of thirty to ninety years in prison by the District of Columbia court. However, along the way, several of Kent's constitutional rights were violated. Among other things, his lawyer was not allowed to see certain documents that would have helped in his case. Also, the juvenile judge did not inform Kent as to why he was going to be tried in an adult court. His case was appealed all the way to the United States Supreme Court in 1966, and the Supreme Court ruled in his favor by overturning the Washington, D.C., court's decision. "The U.S. Supreme Court wanted the Kent Decision to ensure that juveniles could not be waived to adult criminal court for trial without a formal hearing before a judge and with the assistance of a lawyer."[13]

In Re **Gault.** The second Supreme Court case, the most widely known, was the case of Jerry Gault, who changed a large part of the juvenile justice system with a phone call. In 1964, Gault, who was fifteen years old at the time, and his friend Ron Lewis allegedly made an obscene phone call to an elderly woman in their neighborhood in Globe, Arizona. The woman called the county sheriff's office and filed a complaint. The officers

The Supreme Court building in Washington, D.C., is home to the highest court in the United States.

picked up Gault and brought him before a juvenile court judge. During the two hearings that he had, Jerry was not permitted to have a lawyer with him. He was told that he did not have the right to remain silent, and the woman, Mrs. Cook, was not required to testify in court. The juvenile court judge sentenced Jerry Gault to the Arizona State Industrial School for six years until he reached the age of twenty-one. Gault's parents hired a lawyer who appealed the decision of the juvenile court judge. In 1967, the case was heard before the United States Supreme Court.

In a landmark Supreme Court decision known as In re *Gault*, Justice Abe Fortas, speaking for eight of the nine members of the Court, said, "Under our Constitution the condition of being a boy does not justify a kangaroo court." Justice Fortas meant that young people like Jerry Gault had the same rights as adults under the due process clause of the Fourteenth Amendment of our Constitution. The Supreme Court said that Jerry and his parents had to be made aware of the charges against him. It also stated that Gault had the right to have a lawyer at any time during his questioning and his hearing and if the Gaults could not afford a lawyer, the court would appoint one for them. The decision also stated that Gault, and all juveniles, were protected by the Fifth Amendment of the Constitution, giving him the right to remain silent. Finally, the juvenile court was required to keep accurate written records. As a result of the *Gault* decision, Jerry Gault was set free.[14]

A series of other Supreme Court cases since the *Gault* decision have dealt with the legal rights of juveniles. The

1970 case of twelve-year-old Samuel Winship was particularly important. The Supreme Court ruled that there should be a difference in the burden of proof in cases regarding juveniles. As a result, there must be proof "beyond a reasonable doubt" in both adult and juvenile cases.[15] (Prior to this decision, juveniles could be judged guilty without a jury trial.)

There are, however, those who feel that juvenile court judges today are too soft on youthful offenders. Because of the sharp increase in juvenile crime, there has been a public demand for stronger prosecution of violent juvenile offenders and more transfers to the adult court system. In fact, from 1979 to 1984, the number of juveniles sent to adult prisons increased by 48 percent. What is behind this increase in juvenile crime? The next chapter explores some of the reasons why so many young people, such as the juveniles described above, commit crimes.

3

What Causes Juvenile Crime?

Why have the young people in America become so violent? Law enforcement and social service agencies are trying to figure out the answer to this question. According to Dean Murphy in "The Rise in Kids Who Kill," which appeared in the *Los Angeles Times*, an FBI report found that "children are killing more than ever."[1]

Many law enforcement officials feel that juvenile crime—especially crimes against property—is on the rise at a faster rate than adult crime. He said that many of the thefts that are being committed now are by teens who are on drugs or looking for money to buy them.[2]

There are many differing opinions about the cause of this increase in juvenile crime. No one single reason can be cited for the increase, rather many causes combine and contribute to cause it.

Youth Gangs

A gang is a group of people who get together to take part in illegal activities. Many young people today feel that they need to be part of a group, to know that there are people who care about them. Juvenile gangs offer peer support if someone "disses" a fellow gang member. Gang members, whose ages can range from eight to forty-five, show their affiliation by wearing certain clothing, a special symbol, or a special color. The city of Los Angeles is believed to have six hundred gangs with over seventy thousand members. The most notorious, the "Crips" and the "Bloods," are rival African-American street gangs and have official gang colors. Gangs in other cities have sprung up using the same names and trying to imitate those in Los Angeles.

Many gang members will kill to defend the honor of the gang or to protect "turf" or friends. They often kill for the most ridiculous reasons. One young gang member said that he shot his barber because he did not like the haircut he got. Gangs often prey on students by robbing and attacking them on their way to school.

Another factor that has led to the increase in gang violence is the springing up of the hate group or "skinhead" gangs. Instead of targeting rival gangs or neighborhoods, these gangs target minority groups such as Asian Americans, African Americans, Jews, and gays and lesbians. They specifically take aim at groups that are different from them.

Cities with some of the most severe gang problems include New York, Los Angeles, Chicago, Detroit, Philadelphia, and San Francisco. Yet gang activities are not just limited to big cities. In Burlington City, New Jersey, near Camden, officials have recently completed a two-and-a-half-month investigation of gangs in their town. They have been able to identify five gangs operating in the neighborhood. The gangs have names like "Backdoor" and "Frontline." As a result of the police and the community working together, eleven people were arrested, two of them juveniles. Four others are still being sought. In the last year and a half, there have been thirty violent crimes in this area. Police hope that this crackdown will send a message and help to ease the gang problem.[3] Even though gangs have been around for two centuries, they seem to be more violent and more deadly today than ever before. Many gang members have little respect for human life.

Guns

The easy accessibility of guns and the willingness of young people to use them without hesitation is another of the causes of juvenile violence. "By 1990, there were probably more than 20 million guns in private hands in the United States and around half of American households contained a gun."[4] Between 1985 and 1994, the arrest rate for juveniles between ages ten and seventeen in weapons violations increased 103 percent.[5] In America's schools, it is estimated that as many as one hundred thousand students carry guns to school on any given day.

The ability to obtain guns easily has made gang membership more violent and potentially more dangerous. In Washington, D.C., for example, guns can be purchased for prices that range from $20 to $200. Everything from a .25 caliber pistol to a 9mm semiautomatic is available. In some instances, a person can even rent a gun for one night. Because guns are easy to get and very easy to use, shooting has become a simple way to deal with gang disputes. Just visit a big city hospital emergency ward on a Saturday night and you can see the results of gangs and guns.

Drugs and Alcohol

"Eva" is a sixteen-year-old patient at New York City's Phoenix House drug rehabilitation center who got hooked on crack two years ago. The product of a troubled middle-class family, she was already a heavy drinker and pot smoker when she was introduced to coke by her older brother, a young dope pusher. "When you take the first toke on a crack pipe, you get on top of the world," she says.

She first started stealing from family and friends to support her habit. She soon turned to prostitution and went through two abortions before she was sixteen. "I didn't give a damn about protecting myself," she said. "I just wanted to get high. Fear of pregnancy didn't even cross my mind when I hit the sack with someone for drugs."[6]

The United States has the highest rate of teen drug use in the industrialized world. Some studies show that between 60 and 90 percent of all juvenile crime in our country is drug related. "One out of every three twelve- to seventeen-year-olds has tried marijuana. . . . Almost one in every five high school seniors has tried cocaine or

Juvenile gangs, like this one, are a dangerous problem for cities and towns in the United States.

crack." This widespread teen drug abuse is thought to be the cause of many of the violent crimes in this country. Drug use by gangs is a particularly disturbing factor.[7]

The average age of first time use of alcohol is twelve. For drug use it is thirteen. In 1986, there were more than two hundred fifty thousand juvenile arrests for drug and alcohol offenses. A survey completed the following year showed that "almost 48 percent of youth under 18 in long term, state operated juvenile institutions were under the influence of alcohol at the time of committing the offense they were arrested for."[8] Many of those arrests were for drunk driving and for causing fatal accidents. Of that number, police arrested three times as many boys as girls. As drugs became more difficult to buy, teen drinking began to increase. Even though it is illegal for minors to buy liquor, they do not seem to have any trouble getting adults to buy it for them. According to Detective Mike Brogan of the Lower Township, New Jersey, Police Department, local liquor stores are some of the first places he checks on his evening rounds, especially on weekends and during the summer months. This is to be sure that juveniles are not hanging around waiting for an adult to buy beer or liquor for them.

Many teens have experimented with using drugs and alcohol together. This mixture can lead to overdosing and even death. Teenagers say that the reason they do this is to get high, feel good, and be accepted by their friends. They use drugs and drinking to fight boredom or because they see other members of their families doing it. They also say it is glamorous and is often shown in movies and on television.[9]

Up to 10 percent of juveniles involved in drugs may be drug dealers. Teen drug dealers are often connected to gang and school violence, two environments where drug sales and use are part of the way of life.

Entertainment and the Media

There are many teachers and sociologists who say that one of the leading causes of juvenile crime is that there is too much violence on television and in the movies. Young people are often left alone while their parents are working, so there is little or no control over the programs they watch. Children, especially younger children under the age of ten, like to imitate what they see. Some experts in child development feel that children as young as fourteen months can imitate the behaviors they see on television. Our society has continued to allow more and more violence on television and in the movies. In a recent survey done by a national news magazine, 90 percent of the people who answered said that violence in the movies and on TV was still a serious problem.

Many of our government leaders feel the same way. President Bill Clinton has accused the entertainment industry of "incessant, repetitive, mindless violence and irresponsible conduct."[10] His daughter, Chelsea, a teenager, is concerned about the shows and movies she watches. Former Senate Majority Leader Robert Dole is also worried about the issue of violence. He said that Hollywood "poisons the minds of our young people . . . with destructive messages of casual violence. . . ."[11] Attorney General Janet Reno has warned television and film producers to cut down on violence or the federal government may have to step in to regulate the industry.

Both television and movies in the United States glorify violence. By watching some of their action heroes like the Power Rangers, children get the message about the "good" that can result from violent actions. These violent actions are also portrayed in the comic books that young people buy. A recent study showed that cartoon violence has become quite common on the Saturday morning shows. Fights between characters is the main attraction for those children who watch them.

According to Professor J. D. Halloran of Leicester University in Great Britain, "children who are more aggressive to start with tend to be less popular with their age mates and are likely to spend more time alone watching television."[12] Shows like *Top Cops* and *Unsolved Mysteries* have become prime-time favorites. Other shows such as *Inside Edition* and *Hard Copy* also portray violent acts.

A study done in Great Britain on the effects that television has on violent behavior pointed to the fact that both the shows and the people of the United States were more violent than their counterparts in Britain and added that "there can be no doubt that television and delinquent behavior can be regarded as a social problem in the United States."[13] America is "a society where young children watch an average of 25 hours of television per week—with 5 violent acts an hour during prime time and 26 an hour on Saturday morning."[14]

Even today's pop music is being pointed to as a contributor of violence. One whole segment of the music industry, called gangsta rap, has been particularly blamed. Artists like Tupac Shakur (who was recently killed in a violent shooting), 2 Live Crew, Ice-T, and Intelligent Hoodlum perform songs with lyrics that encourage murder and the abuse of women. Songs with titles like "Bullet in the Brain" and "Cop Killer" are just some examples of the rap music that has invaded our culture. Two recording companies, Geffen Records and the rap music division of Time Warner, are taking a long look at the albums they are currently producing. KPRS in Kansas City, Missouri, is one radio station that has decided to no longer play rap that is violent or sexually explicit.[15]

Lack of Supervision/ Single-Parent Homes

Working parents and single-parent families have given rise to the latchkey generation—a group of children who are often left unsupervised after school, on weekends, and during the summer months. Free time becomes the prime opportunity for young people to get into trouble. According to FBI statistics, violent crimes committed by juveniles occur most often between the hours of 3:00 P.M. and 6:00 P.M., coinciding with the end of the school day and the early evening.[16] The following story is an example of what can happen when children are left alone.

Natavia Moore, age ten, was at home taking care of her two brothers and a cousin in their house in Fort Lauderdale, Florida. Her father was at a friend's house and her mother was away on a cruise. Natavia had been jealous of her younger brother Desmond. While they were playing Nintendo, Natavia found her father's gun and shot her younger brother in the head. He was taken to a hospital and needed brain surgery. Natavia is being held at a detention center in Florida. Her father could also be subject to arrest. Florida law states that if a loaded weapon is left within easy reach of anyone under age sixteen and if anyone is injured because of it, the owner of the gun could be charged with a crime. The punishment can be up to five years in prison and a fine of $5,000.

This incident might not have happened if an adult or responsible teenager had been present to supervise the children. Children as young as Natavia should not be taking care of other children.[17]

Minority Crime

There are those who believe that the cycle of violence has its roots in the way that minorities have been treated in this country since its beginning. Fox Butterfield, a writer for *The New York Times*, recently wrote a book entitled *All God's Children*. In it he talks about Willie Bosket, who at the age of fifteen murdered two people on the subway in New York City. Bosket, now age thirty-two, is serving time at the Woodbourne Correctional Center in New York. He still has seventy-five years to serve on his sentence.

Butterfield's book traces violence back to the South during the era of slavery before the Civil War. He tells how violent and corrupt society was. Slave families who were mistreated, according to Butterfield, carried their anger with them when they gained freedom. The rage of the past centuries lives on.

As you can tell from this chapter, there is no single cause of juvenile crime that we can point to. This makes it difficult to try to find solutions. Social changes like the change in the family structure will probably not reverse to the lifestyle of past eras. Tougher laws, however, can be passed to try to control the easy availability of guns. As for the entertainment industry, it will be up to parents and lawmakers to set the standards of what is appropriate for young people to see. In the next chapter we will examine how the juvenile justice system works when a young person commits a crime.

4

How the Juvenile Justice System Works

Our juvenile justice system is different from the adult criminal justice system in the way it deals with offenders. The main goals of the juvenile justice system are to convict those who have committed crimes and to prevent them from committing further crimes. Another goal is to try to keep young people out of juvenile court when possible, and out of the adult criminal justice system. Back in 1970, Milton Luger, then the director of New York State's Division for Youth, said, "It would probably be better for all concerned if young delinquents were not detected, apprehended, or institutionalized. Too many of them get worse under our care."[1] But the truth is that now more juveniles are being arrested and sent through the justice system than ever before. Several programs have been developed to try to separate the juveniles from the formalized juvenile justice system. They are called diversion programs, and they deal with juveniles in a more informal and less threatening way than the court system does.

The crimes most juvenile offenders commit fall under state law jurisdiction. We will look at a typical state juvenile justice system, that of New Jersey.

Custody

Taking a juvenile into custody is not the same as an arrest. A juvenile can be taken into custody by an order or warrant from a court. He or she can also be taken into custody for delinquency even if a warrant is not issued by a court. In the state of New Jersey, the Department of Corrections determines the place where a juvenile can be detained.

Diversion

Diversion is a program used by the juvenile justice system to move cases away from formal processing to other services run by social agencies or the juvenile court.[2] Most of the recommendations for diversion come from the local police departments. Local police officers are the real keys to the success of the juvenile justice program in the United States. When a juvenile is taken into custody, the juvenile officers must decide in which direction to send the case. In some states, there are special programs run by the schools, local governments, or the communities. One of these programs is the Juvenile Conference Committee.

The Juvenile Conference Committee is used as a diversion program. It has been used in the state of New Jersey for several years. The committee is designed to

Early in this century, juvenile convicts often worked in the fields as part of their sentence.

help juveniles who have committed minor offenses and who have gotten into trouble for the first time. It is part of a plan to reduce caseloads in the juvenile courts.

The program is run by the Family Division of the Superior Court. These conference committees usually have between six and nine members, who have been appointed by the Family Division Judge. This judge also appoints the chairperson, whose term runs for three years. The adults who are chosen for the committee are concerned citizens who live in the community. When selected, they attend training sessions to learn how the program operates. Police officers, school board members, and certain other individuals are not allowed to serve. Cases are referred to the committee by intake officers. Such cases may include thefts of less than $200, shoplifting, trespassing, minor drug possession, and driving a car without a license.

Juvenile offenders and their parents or guardians are asked to attend a meeting on a specific date and time. Most of these meetings are held in schools or municipal buildings. Before the meeting, the committee members review the incident, as well as the juvenile's record. They then meet with the juvenile and the victim individually. After the initial meeting, the conference committee makes suggestions and recommendations that will be presented at a second meeting. They take into consideration the age of the juvenile, the severity of the offense, and the juvenile's previous record.

Some of the possible outcomes of a juvenile conference hearing can be:

1) a written apology to the victim

2) an essay

3) community service

4) repayment for damaged or stolen goods

5) counseling

If the conference meetings are not successful or if the juvenile refuses to follow its recommendations, then the case can be returned to the court. If a crime is serious enough or if the juvenile is a repeat offender, a case will go through the legal system and not the conference committee.[3]

What Is Juvenile Intake?

If a juvenile is arrested by the local police department, one of several things may happen. This operation varies from state to state. At some point in the process, the juvenile may be taken to juvenile court intake. Here, a determination is made as to whether a petition should be filed against a juvenile. A petition is filed if the charge is serious enough to proceed through the justice system. It is up to the intake officer rather than the prosecutor to decide if a petition should be filed for action by the court. If the case does go to court, then probable cause must be established. Intake officers also explain to the youth what his or her legal rights are.

Detention Centers

Most juvenile delinquency cases do not involve detention. There are, however, over four hundred juvenile detention centers in the United States to be used when detention is called for. A juvenile may be placed in a detention facility at several points in his or her legal proceedings. The most common reasons for detention placement are if the youth is a threat to the neighborhood, if there is a likelihood that he or she will not appear at the hearing, or if the juvenile is a threat to himself or herself.[4]

For many juvenile offenders these centers are their first taste of life in a restricted, prison-type environment. Local police departments say that they do not have enough officers to watch, all day and all night, all of the youths that have been taken into custody. Many youths are sent to detention facilities that are so overcrowded that some young offenders may be sent to facilities in other counties.

While in detention facilities, juveniles receive a health screening and medical care if required. Arrangements are also made for juveniles to continue to receive their education. Parents and family are usually permitted to visit juveniles in detention. Phone calls and mail, although regulated, are also allowed.

Some juveniles accused of less serious crimes are often sent to local youth shelters that are used mostly for runaways or battered children. Others are just sent back to their homes.

Operating detention facilities is expensive. The cost

of running them, along with running training schools for juvenile offenders, is about $1 billion a year.

What Does a Juvenile Court Do?—The Adjudication Process

The trial stage in the juvenile justice process is called the adjudication phase. Here, charges are presented and the juvenile and his or her attorney are given the opportunity to state their side of the story. If found guilty, the youth may receive a sentence that may be probation, community service, or placement in a state institution. "Less than one third of all court referrals are formally adjudicated."[5]

The operation of the juvenile court system varies from state to state. In some states, like New York, they are called family courts. Elsewhere they are considered to be parts of other courts. Juvenile courts are not meant to be like adult criminal courts. Most have no juries. There are no federal juvenile courts. Generally, juvenile court sessions are not open to the public or the media, and juvenile court records may be sealed.

"The original goals of the juvenile courts were based on the concept that children needed the state to act as a kindly parent to protect them from the severity of adult courts and penal institutions."[6] Juvenile (or family) courts also try to change the behavior of young people so that they will not commit any more crimes. It often turns out that the juvenile (or family) court system is a last-resort government agency for young people in trouble.

The police or intake officers sometimes determine whether a juvenile case should go to court. Other times

Youth shelters, which previously gave shelter to runaways and homeless youths, are now also used as detention centers.

the decision is made by the prosecutor. When a case does go to court, there are many things to be considered by the judge before making this decision:

1) Does the juvenile have a prior record?

2) What type of crime was committed?

3) How does the victim feel about the case?

4) What is the family situation of the offender?

5) What programs have been available in the community to help the juvenile?

6) How does the accused juvenile respond to the police?

7) Is the juvenile detention center overcrowded?[7]

If the crime is a serious one or if the juvenile has been to juvenile court before, the judge may decide to transfer or "waive" the case to a regular adult criminal court.

Interviews with two juvenile court judges, one from a large city and one from a more rural suburban area, give us an idea of what it is like to work with young people in trouble.

Judge David B. Mitchell was an associate judge of the Baltimore, Maryland, City Circuit Court. In an interview for *Juvenile Justice Magazine* he talked about what it was like to be a juvenile court judge. He said, "When you sit in the juvenile court, you have the opportunity to speak to the broader social problems of your community and to really participate in making things better overall. . . ."[8] Many juvenile courts use nonjudges as referees to handle less serious cases and to lighten the burden for the judges. But Judge Mitchell feels that judges need to be involved in the ultimate decisions affecting juveniles. Mitchell also believes that only juvenile court judges should make the decision of transferring or "waiving" a juvenile into adult court. He feels that the waiver is used too much. This may be partly due to the current public frustration with juvenile violence and the outcry for stricter punishments when dealing with juvenile offenders. This is especially true in the large cities. In Maryland, "if a child is sixteen years of age or older and is charged with a handgun offense, the juvenile court does not have any jurisdiction in that case."[9]

When asked about putting juveniles in prison, Judge Mitchell said,

> If putting people in penitentiaries for decades was effective, we wouldn't have gotten to this stage. Incarceration (imprisonment) does not work. What imprisonment accomplishes, at the juvenile or adult level, is removal of that person from society. . . . Unfortunately it is not a deterrent.[10]

Many juvenile offenders are truants, young people who often avoid going to school. Judge Mitchell said that 30 percent of the elementary pupils in Baltimore are chronic truants who miss at least six weeks of school a year. It seems that almost every person who comes before the juvenile and adult criminal system has either dropped out of school or failed to attend.

Judge Raymond Batten is the superior court judge who handles juvenile cases in the southern part of New Jersey. In an interview, he explained his efforts to make young people aware of juvenile proceedings and what can happen to teens. He allows students to visit his courtroom. Tuesday is the day he devotes to juvenile issues. As long as the cases are appropriate for the public to attend, Judge Batten will permit students to watch the hearings. He even stops the proceedings to explain what is going on to the visitors. By educating many of the area's students, Judge Batten feels that he can help to reduce juvenile crime in his county.

Probation

If a juvenile is found to be delinquent, or guilty of an offense, he or she may be placed on probation. This is a widely used procedure in dealing with juveniles who have gotten in trouble with the law. Even though it is the oldest part of our juvenile justice system, probation is still used by many communities today. One of the goals of probation is to provide a wide variety of services to help young offenders deal with their problems. It is less expensive than other alternatives and avoids sending a juvenile to an institution.

Conditions for probation vary from state to state. These conditions may include staying out of trouble or may require more specific behavior, such as going to school regularly, being home by curfew, not possessing weapons, not drinking or using drugs. A juvenile may be placed in a foster home or be required to complete community service as part of the probation. If a juvenile or his or her parents violate the conditions of probation, the case may be sent back to court.[11] During the period of probation, an offender remains in his or her community and is encouraged to continue with work or education.

A young person on probation can still stay in the neighborhood, but he or she is under the supervision of a probation officer. This officer works for the juvenile court and is like a counselor. Juveniles who are placed on probation must report to the probation officer regularly. The probation officer's job is to counsel young offenders with the hope that they will not commit crimes again. The probation officer must also keep accurate records of the case and be aware of what the juveniles are doing.

In some states, such as Pennsylvania, probation officers have been placed in the local public schools. They check up on the juvenile offenders' attendance. If the juveniles are not in school, the officers may go to their homes and bring them to school. Because these probation officers work in the school building, they are able to see students every day. The probation department and school officers can work together to best help young people to be more successful and stay out of trouble.

Probation is not suitable for all cases. In some instances, the crime is serious and probation is not even allowed by the law. Sometimes, people in the neighborhood feel that probation is not a severe enough penalty. They will demand a stricter punishment.

Institutionalization

A key question of juvenile justice programs has always been where to place juveniles in trouble. Correctional facilities have been less than pleasant, and are often dangerous. Some are very similar to adult prisons while others seem more homelike. The staff members who work in these institutions are often hardworking and dedicated employees who have been trained to help young people in trouble.

Correctional facilities got their start in England where Bridewell's, the first house of corrections, was built in the 1500s. These institutions, which started out as places for homeless and runaway children, have become holding tanks for violent as well as unwanted young people. In 1990, over ninety-seven thousand young people in the United States were admitted to public correctional facilities.[12] Let us take a look at the various placements that are available for juvenile offenders. But keep in mind this question: Can placing a juvenile in a prison or training school for a long time change his or her behavior?

One of the least restrictive placements is a group home, halfway house, or shelter. These homes were started back in 1916, in an attempt to keep young people out of prisons. They are also used for children who cannot go back to their own homes. In many cases a poor home situation caused the juvenile to commit a crime. Usually, between six and fifteen residents live in a group home. Most group homes are privately run.

Other juveniles may be placed in a foster home for a year or more. The host family is usually paid by the state for taking care of the child. Children who have the need for both adult supervision and a substitute parent are often placed in foster homes by the juvenile court.

Several other institutions have been developed over

the years to house juvenile offenders. They include reform schools, training schools, youth camps, ranches, and juvenile prisons. According to a 1991 survey, 75 percent of juveniles held in long-term facilities were held in training schools.[13] The purpose of these long-term facilities is to punish the juvenile, remove him or her from the community, and reduce the juvenile's chances of future delinquent behavior.

These are the places of last resort for juvenile offenders. But if most of the facilities are like adult prisons, how are we to expect them to work? There have been reported cases of violence, sexual abuse, and drug use in juvenile facilities. Punishments that include medication and isolation have also been used in juvenile facilities.[14] Placement in facilities can also be very expensive, costing as much as $35,000 per child for a year.

Parole

Sometimes juveniles will be released from institutions before their full sentence is served. This is called parole. This may be done for any one of several reasons, including good behavior in the institution. The juvenile is returned to his or her community under the supervision of a parole officer. This is part of what is known as aftercare. The juvenile is responsible for checking in with his or her parole officer on a regular basis in order to let the officer know how he or she is doing both in school and in the neighborhood. If the parolee is arrested during this time, parole can be revoked, and the parolee can be returned to detention. It is hoped that by sending a young person back home under certain conditions, he or she will not return to his or her criminal ways.

Transfer to Criminal Court

If a juvenile is charged with a serious crime (murder, rape, armed robbery), has a long prior record, or has not responded to efforts to help, then he or she may be transferred or waived to criminal court. Recently there has been a fairly large increase in the number of cases sent to adult court. Between 1988 and 1992, the number of these transfers increased 68 percent.[15] Most of these cases involved drug-law violations and crimes against property.

5

Juvenile Crime: A View From Two Cities

A day in the life of juvenile police officers in large cities can be very different from those in a small town. There is more potential for violence in big cities, especially with juvenile gangs. Interviews with two police officers, Detective Mike Brogan of Lower Township, New Jersey, and Lieutenant Daniel Placentra of the Philadelphia Police Department, illustrate the differences as well as the similarities of their jobs.

Detective Michael Brogan* is a twenty-five-year veteran of the Lower Township Police Department in New Jersey. He is a graduate of the eleven-week police training academy program at Sea Girt, New Jersey. His first assignment was as a patrol officer in the department. He was later assigned to the detective bureau because of his intuitive and investigative ability, as well as his rapport with people. His main task was to perform criminal

---

* Detective Brogan has retired since the time of his interview with the author of this book.

investigations. Early in his career there was no formal or separate department to deal with young people.

Brogan received special training from the FBI in arson investigation and hostage negotiation. He then briefly returned to patrol work. For the last five years he has been assigned to the detective section in the juvenile bureau. At this time Brogan was trained to be a D.A.R.E. (Drug Abuse Resistance Education) officer. This is a national program to develop drug awareness in elementary school children. His most recent responsibilities are to investigate cases of sexual abuse and child sexual assault as well as juvenile crime. Brogan regularly visits the neighborhoods in this community of more than thirty square miles. When not in uniform, he contributes to the youth of his community in other ways. He is an umpire for the local Little League and serves on the board of education of the Lower Cape May Regional School District. He feels that it is important to be active in the community and make one's presence felt in positive ways as a deterrent to juvenile crime.[1]

Juvenile Crime in a Major City

Lieutenant Daniel Placentra has been with the Philadelphia Police Department for thirty-six years. During those years, he has spent much of his of time dealing with the city's juveniles. Placentra is currently in charge of the police department's gang unit. He also deals with missing juveniles and the city's graffiti problem.

In a recent interview, Lieutenant Placentra and Detective Steven Cooke talked about the current juvenile crime problem in Philadelphia. Placentra said that while holdups and burglaries were on the decline, there was a major rise in weapons offenses as well as aggravated assaults. He said it was too easy for young people to get guns and knives.[2]

When asked what he thought were the major reasons for the increase in juvenile crime, Lieutenant Placentra cited two causes. One is the disintegration of the family unit. He said that "young people today lack the support that both the family and the neighborhood used to provide."[3] Placentra also said that sometimes when he calls parents to inform them that the police have their child in custody, some of the parents don't even want to come to the station to get their children. Other parents refuse to believe that their children could have done anything wrong.

Another concern that Lieutenant Placentra had was about the way juveniles are treated by the legal system. He feels that judges are too easy on juvenile offenders and this often sends the wrong message to young offenders and encourages them to go out and commit crime again. He added that sometimes the police department feels powerless. He cited instances when police spend a great deal of investigative work trying to solve a crime, only to have the juvenile released because of a legal technicality.

When asked about gangs, Placentra said that "we cannot wipe gangs out. We just want to keep them under control." Two areas of the city that are gang turfs are the local playgrounds and the housing projects. Police monitor these areas to prevent gang violence and drinking. "When we go out to a housing project," Placentra said,

Juvenile crime is usually more violent in large cities. These teens were arrested after allegedly mugging an individual in a New York City subway.

"we have to send three patrol cars. One officer guards the cars while the other two investigate the incident."

Placentra offered a parting piece of advice for parents: "Never let your children leave the house angry."[4]

A Night on the Street With Detective Brogan—Small-Town Problems

It is late on a Friday afternoon in August. There will be a full moon tonight. The temperature is above 90 degrees and the people on and along the shore are preparing for another weekend and another heat wave. Detective Brogan is working the 2:00 P.M. to 10:00 P.M. shift. However, he is on call until Monday morning.

Brogan checks his log to see what cases were entered and are still pending since he was last in his office. He then checks the department computer. Two incidents have occurred. One concerned a thirteen-year-old girl who allegedly was assaulted by her father. The girl was taken to the local hospital to determine if there were any injuries. The father was questioned and released. The Division of Youth and Family Services of New Jersey will be informed about the incident. Detective Brogan informs me that charges will be filed against the father in a few days.[5]

The second case involved a fight that broke out at a party. A group of uninvited teenagers, who had been drinking, crashed the party. The incident included the throwing of beer bottles and trash cans. Several windows were smashed. One seventeen-year-old boy received a severe gash on his arm that required major plastic surgery. No arrests were made.

Lower Township, New Jersey, encompasses a broad

area that includes several major highways, residential and commercial neighborhoods, and undeveloped woods. There is also a stretch of land along the Delaware Bay with vacation homes and the dock for the Cape May-Lewes Ferry. There are senior citizen complexes and low-income housing. There are also several campgrounds that are opened during the summer months. It was along these areas that we began our patrol.

During our tour of this community of twenty thousand residents, Brogan remarked that there is not a lot for young people to do. There is no place for them to go. Transportation to the recreation center is often a problem for many of the teens. This boredom can later turn into trouble. But he remarks that it has been unusually quiet this summer.[6]

Detective Brogan also talks about the changes in the community. He says while most of the juvenile crimes committed have been against property (shoplifting, vandalism, and so on) rather than against people, there has been an increase in violent crimes. More youths are becoming more physical because "their moral values are lessening and kids are becoming more territorial. They will fight to keep things."

Brogan does not, however, believe that organized gangs have become a major threat in the community. The one gang that did come into the area went on to more promising turf when casino gambling came to Atlantic City. Brogan, like Lieutenant Placentra of Philadelphia, attributes much of the nationwide rise in juvenile crime to the decline of the family. He points out that there are a large number of single-parent families in this community.[7]

Patrol Log

A typical evening for a juvenile officer patrolling a town like Detective Brogan's might include the following:

6:30 P.M. We received a call regarding four juveniles, three girls and a boy, apprehended on the beach with a possible controlled dangerous substance in their possession. One of the girls collapsed while being questioned by police. By the time we arrived on the scene there were three police cars and an ambulance. The rescue squad was called, and when her parents arrived, the girl was taken to the hospital for observation. The other youths were questioned, and it was determined that they had purchased a small quantity of marijuana the night before in a nearby town and were smoking it in crude pipes made from aluminum foil. It was decided that no arrests would be made, but the investigating officer would contact all of the parents of the juveniles involved.

7:00 P.M. We were instructed to return to police headquarters to deal with another matter. Two juvenile boys, age sixteen, were picked up by police following a complaint made by the parent of a twelve-year-old. One of the sixteen-year-olds allegedly demanded money from the younger boy and threatened to beat him if he did not give it to him. The young boy said he had none. The alleged robber then threatened to hurt the boy even worse if he did find money in his pocket. The younger boy gave up his money and fled home on his bicycle. This crime is known as a strong-arm robbery and is a serious offense in New Jersey.

A computer check on the sixteen-year-old indicated a prior arrest record that included shoplifting at a local discount store. The boy was photographed and fingerprinted. His parents were then contacted. No one was allowed to question him until his parents arrived. If he or his parents wanted a lawyer at that time, they would be allowed to have one. Meanwhile, down the hall, the victim, accompanied by his parents, was completing a statement.

Detective Brogan instructed the officer on the case to contact the county juvenile intake bureau. He recommended that the juvenile be placed in a detention facility. However, there were several problems. Cape May County does not have its own juvenile facility, and therefore must rely on a facility in a neighboring county. Cape May has been allotted only five beds in this facility. If all of the beds were being used, the youth would have to be released to his parents.

If detention were possible, he would be transported by the sheriff's department to the juvenile facility and committed until Monday morning, at which time he would have a hearing before a juvenile judge. However, if a more serious crime were committed by someone else between now and then, the boy could be released from the facility and sent home. When we left the station, the police were waiting for his parents. It was now dark, and Detective Brogan returned to his car and headed to those hideout spots where juveniles like to go on weekends to drink and take drugs.

To meet the growing demands of the community, the Lower Township Police Department has expanded from about seventeen officers in 1974 to its current fifty officers. They have also placed officers in the local elementary schools, the junior high school, and the regional high school. These officers, known as school resource officers, resolve conflicts between students, check up on truant students, and monitor visitors in the building.[8]

A Juvenile Is Apprehended

Officer Brogan used a real case to illustrate how the system works with juveniles in New Jersey. Robert, a fifteen-year-old student at the local high school, has just been discovered with a butterfly knife on school property. A complaint has been filed by the school principal. Here is what takes place.

A police cruiser arrives at the school to take Robert to the station. Immediately, by law, Robert's parent or guardian must be notified. The police may not question him or say anything until his parent arrives. The parent is notified of the charges. In this case, it is possession of a weapon in school. The police ask Robert's mother, who has arrived at the station, for permission to speak to her son. She has the right to refuse but does not. At this point, Robert is read his Miranda Warnings and signs a card saying that he has heard them. This means that he knows that he does not have to talk to the police. He may have a lawyer present, and if the family cannot afford one, the court will appoint a public defender. It should be noted that a parent cannot give away a child's rights. Even if Robert's mother said that it was all right for the police to talk to him, Robert could still refuse and could demand an attorney. After Robert signs the card, the police can ask Robert for his side of the story.

Robert is released into the custody of his mother and

his case will eventually be heard in the county juvenile court. If Robert is judged to be delinquent he can be given hours of community service or he can be sent to a juvenile institution. A lot depends on whether this is Robert's first time in trouble or if he has been to juvenile court before.

The Process

Since Robert is older than age fourteen, he can be fingerprinted and photographed. If the child is under that age, a court order is needed. The arresting police officer then types the juvenile complaint. (See p. 65.) At this point, if Robert is not considered dangerous, he is released into the custody of his parent. The local police department then calls the county juvenile intake officer and relates the circumstances of the case. An important decision must now be made. If Robert is an "impact-offender," that is, someone who has had several previous arrests, then he may be placed in detention. If he is to be locked up, a detention hearing must be held within twenty-four hours. At this hearing, the actual charges are not heard. The only issue to be determined is if the juvenile offender should continue to be held in a detention facility. If Robert is sent to the detention facility, the county sheriff sends two deputies who then shackle both his hands and legs and take him away.

Next, the paperwork of Robert's case is sent to the juvenile court, and a hearing is scheduled. This process can take up to three months if Robert is not in detention. Otherwise the process is shorter. Robert is assigned to a

SUPERIOR COURT OF NEW JERSEY
CHANCERY DIVISION, FAMILY PART
COUNTY OF CAPE MAY

Page ____ of ____

COMPLAINT - JUVENILE DELINQUENCY

The State of New Jersey in the Interest of:	Docket number: FJ-___ ___ - ___ ___ ___ ___ ___ - ___ ___ ___ - ___
Mailing address: (Street)	Juv/Party ID number: ___ ___ ___ ___ ___ ___ ___ ___ ___ ___
City, state and zip code:	Name and address of school (and grade) or employer:

Residing in: (township or municipality)	Phone:	Race:	Height:	Weight:
Age:	Date of birth:	Sex:	1 caucasian; 2 black; 3 hispanic; 4 asian/oriental; 5 american indian; 6 other; 7 unknown
AKA:		Color of eyes:	Color of hair:

1. The parent(s) or guardian of the above named juvenile are: (first name, last name)

Address:	Phone:	Relationship:

2. If the above named juvenile is not residing with parent or guardian, he/she is residing with: (name)

Address:	Phone:	Relationship:

Charge No:	The undersigned complainant: (first name, last name)
Of: (identify department or agency)	Address:

says: The above named juvenile is alleged, upon ☐ personal knowledge, ☐ information supplied by others, to be delinquent in that, on or about ___/___/___ at _____ a.m. / p.m. the above named juvenile did: [Set forth facts regarding time, manner, place and the essential elements of the alleged act.]

Co-Defendant(s) Name, Address, and Phone No:

Witness(es) Name, Address, and Phone No:

Violation of (statutory citation and title):

I certify that the foregoing statements made by me are true to the best of my knowledge, information and belief. I am aware that if any of the foregoing statements made by me are willfully false, I am subject to punishment.

Signature of Complainant / Date:	Officer and Department filing police report:

Charge No:	The undersigned complainant: (first name, last name)
Of: (identify department or agency)	Address:

says: The above named juvenile is alleged, upon ☐ personal knowledge, ☐ information supplied by others, to be delinquent in that, on or about ___/___/___ at _____ a.m. / p.m. the above named juvenile did: [Set forth facts regarding time, manner, place and the essential elements of the alleged act.]

Co-Defendant(s) Name, Address, and Phone No:

Witness(es) Name, Address, and Phone No:

Violation of (statutory citation and title):

I certify that the foregoing statements made by me are true to the best of my knowledge, information and belief. I am aware that if any of the foregoing statements made by me are willfully false, I am subject to punishment.

Signature of Complainant / Date:	Officer and Department filing police report:

CP0011 (2/92)

This is a complaint form used for juvenile offenders in New Jersey.

case manager who reviews the case. His case can be treated in three different ways.

The first choice is the Juvenile Conference Committee. As mentioned before, this is a group of local citizens who will meet with the accused and review the circumstances of the case. They cannot administer any punishment. The JCC can, however, assign community service and require restitution (return or payment for stolen or damaged property).

A second alternative is to send the case before a juvenile referee. The referee is a civilian who usually works for the county probation office. He or she acts as a judge and conducts a full hearing into the specific charges of the case. At this hearing, Robert is entitled to all of his rights under the law, including his right to have a lawyer with him. Witnesses can be called. The referee can try the case but does not have the authority to order incarceration (time in prison).

The final alternative is to have Robert's case heard before a juvenile judge. This approach is usually reserved for serious offenses. Legal representation and typed transcripts of the hearing are required. All parties involved give testimony in the case. The judge alone makes the decision. Unlike adult trials there is no jury. Many of the protections and procedures given to Robert in this case came as a result of the U.S. Supreme Court's decision In re *Gault*. A juvenile court hearing is a closed proceeding. It is not open to the general public. The results are so confidential that even the arresting officer may not know the outcome of the case.[9]

6

The Debate: Should Juveniles Be Tried as Adults?

All fifty states permit juveniles to be tried as adults under certain conditions. Some of the states have permitted this since the 1920s. The type of punishment a young offender receives will vary from state to state. As a result, there is wide variation in the harshness of the penalties for committing similar crimes.

The question that must be asked first is "Who is a juvenile?" (See chart on p. 73.) Some states have set the youngest age at which a juvenile can be transferred to an adult court. Other states have no specific age. Many states have laws that allow juveniles to be tried as adults at age sixteen. In Vermont, however, a child of ten can be transferred from juvenile to adult court for committing a major crime. In other states like Arizona, Maine, and Washington, there is no minimum age.[1] In 1993, Colorado, Utah, and Florida made changes in their laws that make it easier to move a juvenile offender to adult court. In Florida, between October 1990 and June 1991, over three thousand youths were transferred to adult court for a wide range of offenses. Some were more serious than others. It seems that the more we read about juvenile violence in the newspaper or see it on television, the more people demand that juveniles be tried and punished like adults in court.[2]

Juveniles Getting Into Adult Court

There are four ways that a juvenile can end up in an adult criminal court. The first is by a juvenile court judge deciding a case is so serious or the number of offenses so many that the juvenile should be transferred to an adult criminal court. In 1992, for example, 11,200 juvenile cases were transferred to criminal court.[3] Second, in several states, the prosecutors are allowed to make the request to move to an adult criminal court. Most often this is done for the same reasons that a judge would use. Third, many states have a specific law that states a juvenile who commits a particular crime, and is of a certain age, must be tried in a criminal court. It is an automatic action. Finally, parents or guardians of the juvenile or the youth himself or herself may request an adult trial. This is usually done if the parents feel that a jury trial will be more fair than a case decided by a juvenile court judge would be. In addition, all of the guaranteed rights that adults have, such as the right to a jury trial or bail, would be extended to the juveniles.

David Freeman, age sixteen, and his brother Bryan, age seventeen, have been accused of murdering their parents and their eleven-year-old brother in February 1995. Their attorneys originally wanted them to be tried as juveniles under the laws of Pennsylvania. However, they recently changed their minds and the brothers will be allowed to be tried as adults. This means that they could both face the death penalty. Both of the brothers have admitted to the killings. However, the lawyers believe they will get a fairer trial with a jury trial than if they were tried as juveniles.[4]

Should a Juvenile Be Tried as an Adult?

In most states the upper age of juvenile court jurisdiction is sixteen. The maximum penalty that a juvenile can receive for any crime is imprisonment until the age of twenty-one. When tried in criminal court the penalties imposed can be the same as those for adults.

The most controversial issue in dealing with juveniles as adults is that of the death penalty. Since colonial days almost three hundred juvenile offenders have been executed for major crimes in the United States. (The courts usually wait until the offender is an adult before carrying out the sentence.) Between 1973 and 1993, 121 death sentences were handed down to young people who were under the age of eighteen when they committed the crime. However, as with adults, a large number of death sentences imposed for crimes committed by juveniles age seventeen or younger have been reversed.[5]

The United States is the only major country that still has a death penalty for juveniles. Canada ended its death penalty for both juveniles and adults in 1976. Many people today feel that capital punishment is a cruel form of

6   PUBLIC LEDGER—PHILADELPI

New House of Detention and Juvenile Court

Ledger
Dec. 10, 1908

Exterior View Of New Structure—22 and Arch Sts.

THIS new building for housing juvenile prisoners has just been completed at 22d and Arch streets. It will be inspected on Saturday afternoon, December 19, when the County Commissioners, the architect and the builders will give a reception and luncheon within its walls.

Recreation Roof For Young Offenders.

A new House of Detention was opened in Philadelphia in 1909.

punishment and ought to be stopped. Fear of the death penalty has not stopped the killings, especially by juveniles. Consider these examples:

> In 1985, while only fifteen years old, Paula Cooper of Indiana stabbed an elderly woman thirty-three times with a butcher knife. She was tried in an adult court and convicted. She was sentenced to die in the electric chair in Indiana.

■ ■ ■ ■

> On May 25, 1986, Jay Pinkerton, who at age seventeen was tried and convicted of raping and murdering a thirty-seven-year-old woman, was executed for this crime. He was twenty-four at the time of his execution. In contrast, fourteen-year-old Matthew Rosenberg raped and drowned a five-year-old boy in Massachusetts. As a result of his crime, he was tried in a juvenile court and sentenced to undergo counseling.[6]

■ ■ ■ ■

Heath Wilkins was also a convicted juvenile murderer. On July 27, 1985, when he was sixteen years old, Wilkins stabbed and killed twenty-seven-year-old Nancy Allen during the robbery of a liquor store in Avondale, Missouri. He used a butterfly knife to repeatedly stab Allen in the chest, heart, throat, and back. When he was arrested, Wilkins was homeless and living in a local playground. A victim of child abuse, he was no stranger to the juvenile justice system. Wilkins pleaded guilty to the crime and requested the death penalty for himself. He told the court that he would prefer the death penalty to a life in prison because "one I fear, the other I don't."[7]

A year and a half after his conviction, Wilkins changed his mind and became part of a United States Supreme Court case appealing the death penalty. On June 26, 1989, the Supreme Court ruled that the death penalty for sixteen- and seventeen-year-olds is not necessarily cruel and unusual punishment and that juveniles may be executed.[8]

A more recent murder case that has drawn national media attention is that of Eric Smith. Smith was a fourteen-year-old who lived in Savona, New York, a town of less than one thousand people. On August 2, 1993, Eric, on the spur of the moment, enticed four-year-old Derrick Robie—who was on his way to a summer day camp program—into a nearby wooded area. According to the police reports, Smith choked the youngster and stuffed a napkin and plastic bag down Derrick's throat. Smith then smashed his head with a rock. Derrick's body was discovered only three hundred yards from his house. When asked why he committed the crime, Smith said, "I don't know." Eric Smith was tried as an adult in a trial with a jury and was found guilty of second degree murder. He was scheduled to remain in a juvenile facility until he turned eighteen and was then transferred to an adult prison.[9]

How a juvenile is treated in a case of murder varies from state to state

What is the minimum age authorized for the death penalty?

Younger than 18	Age 18	None specified
South Dakota (10)[a]	California	Arizona
Arkansas (14)[b]	Colorado	Delaware
Utah (14)	Connecticut[c]	Florida
Virginia (15)	Illinois	Idaho
Alabama (16)	Maryland	Montana
Indiana (16)	Nebraska	Pennsylvania
Kentucky (16)	New Jersey	South Carolina
Louisiana (16)	New Mexico	Washington
Mississippi (16)[d]	Ohio	
Missouri (16)	Oregon	
Nevada (16)	Tennessee	
Oklahoma (16)	Federal System	
Wyoming (16)		
Georgia (17)		
New Hampshire (17)		
North Carolina (17)[e]		
Texas (17)		

Note: Ages at the time of the capital offense were indicated by the offices of the State attorneys general.

a Only after a transfer hearing to try a juvenile as an adult.
b See Arkansas Code Ann. 9-27-318(b)(1) (Repl. 1991).
c See Conn. Gen. Stat. 53a-46a(g)(1).
d Minimum age defined by statute is 13, but effective age is 16 based on an interpretation of U.S. Supreme Court decisions by the State attorney general's office.
e Age required is 17 unless the murderer was incarcerated for murder when a subsequent murder occurred; the age then may be 14.

Source: Greenfeld, L., and Stephen, J. (1993). Capital Punishment 1992. *BJS Bulletin*.

It is very rare for a court to impose the death penalty for a juvenile crime. The United States Supreme Court set sixteen as the minimum age for receiving the death penalty.

Charles Patrick Ewing is a professor at the State University of New York. He wrote a book, *Kids Who Kill*, that describes many brutal juvenile murders of parents, brothers and sisters, friends, and strangers. Ewing feels that most juveniles should be dealt with in a juvenile court. The question that he and many others ask is whether a thirteen- or fourteen-year-old should be held responsible for his or her actions.[10] Does someone that young really know the difference between right and wrong?

In reaction to the crimes of people like Heath Wilkins and Eric Smith, lawmakers throughout the United States have been responding to a public demand for tougher laws for juveniles. As a result, several states have lowered the age at which a person can be tried as an adult. California and Utah are two states that have made changes in their laws. But New York had considered the issue before most others. In 1978, the state legislature passed laws lowering the age at which children can be tried as adults to fourteen for serious crimes like rape and to thirteen for murder cases.[11]

One of the other current arguments about juveniles being treated as adults in court has to do with a juvenile's rights. There are many scholars who feel that juveniles are being treated as second-class citizens by the law and do not have the same rights as adults. The juvenile court judge was supposed to be a sympathetic person who would look out for the best interest of the child with the hope of rehabilitating him or her, but that has not always been the case. Issues like the right to a lawyer, the right to cross-examine witnesses, and the right to establish

There is great disagreement as to whether juveniles convicted of serious crimes should be placed in the same prisons as adults. The major goal of the juvenile justice system should be to help young people get back into society and not commit crimes later as adults.

guilt beyond a reasonable doubt have been fought in the Supreme Court. One issue that is still not settled is a trial by a jury. Juvenile court hearings have no juries.

A Supreme Court decision in 1971, *Mckeiver* v. *Pennsylvania*, said that a jury trial is not required in juvenile cases. The court did write that a juvenile judge could allow a jury trial in certain situations. The use of juries in juvenile trials is permitted by several states. However, when a juvenile is tried as an adult, he or she automatically becomes eligible for a jury trial. No juveniles, however, can serve on these juries. As more young people commit serious crimes, it seems that more will be sent to adult court and will have the right to a jury trial.

There is also a great deal of discussion as to whether juveniles convicted of serious crimes should be placed in the same prisons as adults. Adult prisons are dangerous places. Violence and abuse often occur inside the prison walls. There have also been serious riots in prisons in which adult inmates as well as guards have been killed or injured. If the major goal of juvenile justice is to help young people get back into society and not commit crimes again as adults, are they being cared for most effectively in adult prisons? The case of Pauletta R. is an example of a juvenile court sending a message to juveniles who commit serious crimes without sending juveniles to adult prisons.

Pauletta R. was a fourteen-year-old girl who lived in the Midwest. On July 27, 1991, Pauletta and three girlfriends put together a plan to get $100 to pay off a drug debt that her sister owed. The local gang leader had said that if he did not get the money, he would hurt

Pauletta's sister. Pauletta and her friends decided to pose as prostitutes and try to rob their victims. They lured a man into an alley where a twenty-year-old friend of theirs waited with a gun. A fight broke out, and the man was shot and killed. Pauletta, her girlfriends, and the shooter were charged with first degree murder. The juvenile judge ordered Pauletta to adult court. She was tried and found not guilty of the murder charge but guilty on a charge of armed robbery. She received a sentence of six years at the Illinois Youth Center at Warrenville. She was released in July 1994, after serving four years of her sentence.[12] What is unusual about this case is that although Pauletta was tried as an adult she was placed in a juvenile facility to serve her sentence. Such lengthy sentences are not typical in youth facilities.

Juvenile-court-sponsored programs are designed to help young people get back into the mainstream of society and not commit another crime. If the system has not been working, what can be done?

Many communities are experimenting with new and unusual programs and hope that some of them will help to reduce crime. In the next chapter we will review several programs that are being tried around the country.

7

New and Innovative Programs

People commit crimes for many different reasons. This applies to juveniles as well as adults. The same prevention plan or punishment will not work for every convicted juvenile. In 1978, for example, a research survey showed that sending a juvenile offender to jail had little or no effect in preventing future crimes. The way that young people think has a lot to do with this. According to Jay Albenese, author of *Dealing with Delinquency*,

> If you never think about getting caught, you will never be deterred from committing a crime. Therefore spontaneous acts committed under the influence of alcohol, drugs and acts committed under emotional duress are not deterable. [1]

In 1982, a program, called Scared Straight, was developed in the state of New Jersey using prisoners in jail for life terms. These prisoners acted as teachers to talk about prison and crime to high school students who were at risk for becoming criminals themselves. Many of these students had been in trouble with the police before. This program tried to get young people to understand what could happen to them if they continued to get in trouble. The prisoners used an "in your face" approach, yelling and lecturing to the students. Although the program was featured on television and many news articles were written about it, it was not very successful. Many of the students who took part in the program simply did not feel that they would end up in prison for life.

Not all of the methods used to deal with juvenile crime have resulted in failure. Several states have developed and tried innovative new programs to deal with young people and their problems. Two states, Massachusetts and Utah, have both closed their state training schools and have replaced them with locally based and supported treatment centers. Other states have taken different approaches. An investigation of several of them will show what has been working.

Peer Mediation

In an effort to find peaceful ways to resolve potentially violent problems, schools and towns have started programs called peer mediation. These programs had their beginnings in the 1960s when a program called Teaching Students to be Peacemakers was started at the University of Minnesota. Other states joined in to start similar programs. The Children's Creative Response to Conflict program was begun in New York in the early 1970s to teach nonviolence. A 1977 project in San Francisco was established by Ray Shonholtz, a lawyer.

This program started at the community level and was then tried in the local schools.[2]

In a peer mediation program, students are selected and trained to help classmates work through their problems. Teachers, counselors, and administrators refer students to the mediation program. The mediation team usually consists of two student mediators. They are not allowed to take sides in the cases. They set up the ground rules for mediations and then allow each student to tell his or her side of the story. They try to find some common area that both parties can agree on. At the end of the mediation process, a written agreement is reached and signed by all of the parties. Everything that was said during the mediation is confidential.

One such successful program has been in New Haven, Connecticut. Hillhouse High School is located in that city. Four years ago, in an effort to cut down on arguments and fights in school, a peer mediation program was established. The program is run with the help of the local Community Mediation Center, which trains students to act as mediators to settle disputes between students. About thirty students enrolled in the initial training program, which included about twenty hours of instruction. In these sessions they learn how to resolve arguments by calmly hearing both sides of a story. They learn how to be good listeners. It is very important that the mediators do not get personally involved in the dispute.

The mediators assigned to each session set up the rules for the meeting. The rules include maintaining privacy, avoiding cursing or shouting, and agreeing to the outcome of the mediation.

The New Haven Police Department, as well as officials at the local schools, feel that the program has helped to cut down on fighting in the school. Since some students today carry weapons, it is all too easy for a simple argument to turn into something ugly and violent. Nicholas Pastore, New Haven's Chief of Police, said that the program "has provided people with a real alternative to fighting."[3]

Teen Court

Another experimental program that has met with success around the country is called Trial by Peers or Teen Court. These programs are usually limited to juveniles who have committed offenses like minor traffic violations and shoplifting.

Juveniles who appear in teen court do so voluntarily and give up their right to a regular court appearance and a possible fine or other punishment from the court. If a youth is found guilty in teen court, the sentence may include community service, restitution, counseling, writing essays, or serving on a similar teen court jury. Most of the young people who serve in the court as either lawyers or jury members come from the local schools. The only nonstudent is usually the judge who, in most cases, is a real judge donating his or her time to the program. None of the participants are paid for their work.

If a juvenile offender agrees to participate in and successfully complete the program, his or her record will be expunged (wiped clean) at the end of the sentence.

The G.R.E.A.T. Program teaches school students about the dangers of gang involvement.

(Most of the participants have already pleaded guilty when they enter teen court.) If the judge feels that the penalty is too harsh, he or she has the option to revise the sentence.

Teen court programs have been used in Nevada, Arizona, California, and Texas. At the program in Garland, Texas, only about 10 percent of the juveniles who are eligible for the program get to take part in it. This is partly because the court can hear only a limited number of cases during a session. As the success of these teen court programs becomes more widely known, more cities and towns will probably begin to use them, for several reasons. First, such courts can reduce the burden on the regular court by taking on the more trivial cases. More importantly, they can teach a generation of teenagers how our justice systems works: even though they are legally minors, they are responsible for their actions and will receive consequences for their behavior.[4]

Boot Camps

A new program to introduce a military-style training and discipline into juvenile facilities is being used in several states. It is called "boot camp." These new programs were first started in New Orleans, Louisiana, in 1985. As of 1992, there were only about ten programs throughout the United States.

Although there is a program for girls in Alabama, most of the juvenile boot camps are for boys only. The age range for these programs varies from state to state, but most of them are for youths in the fourteen-year to eighteen-year age range. Most of these programs last for about four months.

Boot camp programs will not usually take someone who has committed a serious violent crime like armed robbery or murder. The goal is to reach a youth that they feel can be rehabilitated to not commit a crime again. Since most of the juveniles in the program are of school age, they must receive at least three hours a day of education. The rest of the time is spent on work projects and military basic training activities. Some states provide drug and alcohol counseling as well as career counseling.

After a boot camp sentence is over, these young adults usually return home where they are checked on by probation or parole officers. Some states have special programs for those who have "graduated" from boot camp.

Since these programs are fairly new, there is not a lot of information available to see how successful they have been or how much money they have cost. There are those who feel that boot camp programs have not been successful. But more states are starting this type of program. Many believe that they can help to reduce juvenile crime, especially with repeat offenders.[5]

A juvenile boot camp program in New York may become the model for other states to follow. The Sergeant Henry Johnson Youth Leadership Academy is located in the Catskill Mountains in the town of South Kortright, New York. It opened in 1992 as New York's first training program for juvenile offenders. This program is open only to boys between the ages of fourteen and seventeen. The residents are youths who have committed acts that are considered adult crimes in New York State. Many of these boys have been convicted of weapons possessions and drug charges. The academy will not accept boys with severe medical or mental problems.

The Youth Leadership Academy, known as the YLA, is a militarylike program run by Colonel Thomas Cornick, who was in the U.S. Army for thirty years. The residents are called "cadets" and wear military uniforms. Their hair is also cut very short like soldiers' hair. The program lasts for six months and is followed by an aftercare program when the boys return to their neighborhoods. The facility can hold up to thirty cadets. Twenty-eight people, who are state employees, work at the academy.

A typical day for the cadets begins at 6:00 A.M. and ends with lights-out at 9:30 P.M. The daily programs include classroom learning, individual counseling, and physical training. The boys have inspection every day before breakfast and are required to scrub the floors and clean the toilets.

Unlike some other juvenile boot camps around the country, YLA works on a system of rewards rather than punishments for changing the youths' behavior. The boys can earn privileges that include reductions in restrictions and field trips to area museums and places of interest.

There is a second part of the academy program that takes place after the cadet leaves the academy facility. It is called the City Challenge Program. This part of the program is in Brooklyn, New York. Cadets are assigned to City Challenge for five days a week for five months. They go to school, and get counseling and job preparation help as well. They also do community service work. At the end of the program, cadets graduate and return to their communities. So far more than 75 percent of the graduates have stayed out of trouble. The cadets who graduated have been very positive. One graduate commented, "When we get out there it's going to be totally different. We're going to be totally different."[6]

The Milton Hershey School

Some of the programs that are getting attention now are not really new. People have become interested in them because they have been successful. Once such place is the Milton Hershey School in Hershey, Pennsylvania. The school was founded by Milton Hershey, the maker of Hershey's candy, and his wife in 1909. The purpose of the school was to provide free education and job training for children (all boys originally) who had a deceased parent. But in the 1960s, the school also began to look for students who were living in poor neighborhood conditions and ran the risk of turning to criminal ways.

Over two hundred new students each year come to the Hershey School. Those who pass the admissions tests are given a place to live, clothing, medical care, and money for college if they graduate from the high school. The school runs from kindergarten to twelfth grade and has a total of more than one thousand students. The grounds cover three thousand acres and include two gyms, a skating rink, and plenty of opportunities to participate in sports.

The school is divided into small cottages where the students live under the eyes of houseparents. Besides going to class, the students have chores to do in their house. The houseparents teach manners and values. They encourage the students to try to be the best they can be.

There are many parents living in dangerous ghettos in the United States who want to get their children out of these dangerous neighborhoods. Many of them try to get their children admitted to the Hershey School, but they are not always successful.

Other states have tried to start live-away schools for teens who are at risk of becoming juvenile delinquents. One school is in Maine; another is in Texas. Both parents and teachers feel that these ideas can be successful in keeping children out of trouble, but the programs are very expensive.[7]

Paint Creek Youth Center

The state of Ohio has developed a residential program to deal with certain juvenile offenders. It is called the Paint Creek Youth Center and is located on a thirty-three-acre site in the southern part of the state. The center, which is privately owned and managed by Lighthouse Youth Services, opened in March 1986 and is available only to boys, age fifteen to eighteen, who have committed a felony (except murder). Those selected must be sent by a county juvenile court judge and the Ohio Department of Youth Services. The offender must not have a serious mental illness.

Paint Creek has two dormitories, a dining hall, a school building, a library, and a recreation area. There are also tennis courts, baseball and football fields, a volleyball court, and a basketball court. There are no high fences or barbed wire. The residents are not in locked cells. The maximum number of residents allowed is thirty-three. There are thirty-one full-time staff members.

The program at Paint Creek is unique in several ways. Residents must pass certain phases of the program to be able to graduate to the next level and eventually to be released. A token system of rewards is used. The young men may earn points for good behavior and level thinking. These points are given out twice a day.

The students receive their education from teachers sent by the Paint Valley School District and are also required to attend special counseling sessions. Here the youths learn about getting along with others and being aware of their behavior. There is a work program that is included along with career training.

The Paint Creek program considers the family to be very important. Family members are asked to participate in treatment and help support the juvenile when he is discharged. After a juvenile is released, a social worker will meet with him to see how he is doing for up to eight months.[8]

Mental Hospitals

Another controversial approach to dealing with less violent juvenile delinquency problems is admitting young people into mental hospitals. Juveniles are locked in places where there may also be adults who are seriously ill. They are labeled as having "conduct disorders." Whether minors agree or not, they can be placed in such places by their parents. This option is used more often for affluent juveniles. Wealthier parents are more likely to have the insurance coverage that will pay as much as $1,000 per day for treatment.

Most of the juveniles in these hospitals are usually guilty of running away from home, cutting school, violating local curfew laws, or disobeying their parents. The treatment for these ailments can include getting medicines or being placed in isolation. Many doctors, educators, law enforcement people, and parents are against this method of dealing with juvenile offenders.[9] Many of these hospitals are found in California, Texas, New Mexico, and Utah.

Prevention Programs

Much of the focus for the prevention of juvenile crime is in the schools. Two programs are in use around the country in both elementary schools and junior high schools. One is the D.A.R.E. program and the other is the G.R.E.A.T. program.

D.A.R.E. (Drug Awareness Resistance Education)

The D.A.R.E. program is an elementary school drug prevention program used to teach young children about the dangers of drugs. In participating towns, one police officer is named the D.A.R.E. officer. The D.A.R.E. program was started jointly by the Los Angeles Police Department and the Los Angeles public schools in 1983. The material was designed to be presented by a uniformed police officer to fifth and sixth grade students

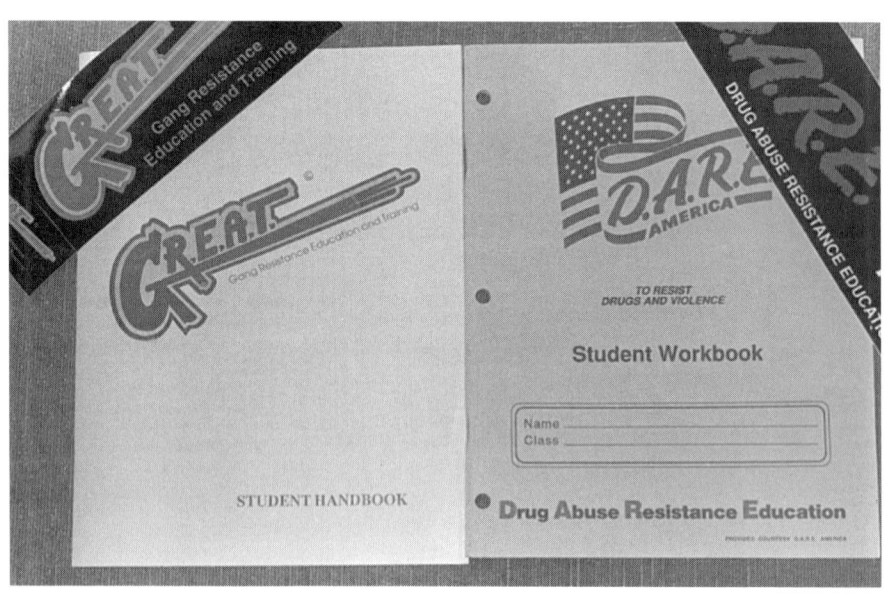

Materials are made available to students to teach them about the dangers of drugs and gangs.

over a seventeen-week period. The program has been so successful that today over half of the school districts in the country are using it. Similar programs dealing with conflict resolution and gang prevention have been modeled after the D.A.R.E. program. Today, D.A.R.E. lessons are being taught to middle and high school students as well as to elementary students.

The G.R.E.A.T. Program

Gangs are found today in many cities and towns of all sizes. Gang members are of all ages and races, and of both sexes. Prosecution and imprisonment have not been able to stop the problem of gang violence in this country. As with other crises, communities have been turning to the schools and the local police for help with gang problems.

The G.R.E.A.T. Program (Gang Resistance Education and Training) is a project supported by the U.S. Bureau of Alcohol, Tobacco, and Firearms along with the Federal Law Enforcement Training Center. Specially trained police officers present a nine-lesson program in the local schools. The lessons include conflict resolution, learning about drugs in the neighborhood, and the effect a crime has on the victim, the victim's family, and the community. The students use role playing and discussions to learn about themselves and what they can do in their schools and the neighborhoods.

This is My Neighborhood—No Shooting Allowed

Judge Jeanne Jourdan is a Superior Court judge in Indiana. Along with community leaders, she developed a program to make neighborhoods safer and to cut down on gun violence by teenagers. Part of the program is designed for the schools. Students are shown a fifteen-minute video in which a shooting incident takes place on a playground. The victim is paralyzed and will have to use a wheelchair for life. The shooter must stand trial in an adult court. The students in the classroom become the jury members who hear the case and then must decide if the accused is guilty of attempted murder or battery, or is not guilty at all.

Other Programs

Sometimes plans to help young people hurt more than help. Such was the case of North Star Expeditions, Inc. This was a wilderness therapy camp in the Utah desert designed for juvenile offenders.

> Sixteen-year-old Aaron Bacon from Phoenix, Arizona, was sent to North Star because of his constant truancy from school and his drug use. He died from a bleeding ulcer while out in the desert on a training exercise. Other such programs have also been cited for injuring residents. Some have closed down, others are under investigation.[10]

There are hundreds of other programs that are being tried all over the country to deal with youth crimes. Large cities, and small towns as well, have to develop new and better ways to reduce juvenile violence. As long as the problem still exists, society will have to continue to develop more ideas to solve it.

Some programs are designed to deal with preventing young people from committing crimes. Programs like peer mediations, D.A.R.E., and G.R.E.A.T. are those types of programs. They have been initiated with the hope that young people can find other ways of solving their problems. Other programs, such as Youth Leadership Academy and Paint Creek Youth Center, are for young people who have already committed serious crimes. They are being treated so that they can return to society and be happy young people who will not get into trouble again.

8

The Future

Hardly a day goes by without a story about another juvenile who has committed a serious crime. The future of the juvenile crime problem does not look very promising. For one thing, the number of young people in this country will increase significantly in the next decade. Between 1990 and 2010, the juvenile population is expected to increase and will reach 74 million. According to the United States Justice Department, "if current trends continue, the number of arrests of juveniles for violent crimes will double by the year 2010."[1] Our public schools, which should be safe places for juveniles under the age of eighteen, will be asked to play the role of referee between students. They will also be called on to teach students about the dangers of drugs and alcohol, as well as gun violence. At one time, teenagers would settle an argument with their fists. Today, they are too quick to use guns.

New Jersey State Senator William Gormley, in an

address to residents at a town meeting in his state, pointed to the problem of a society that does not function.

> The problem is not just the juveniles. If you don't get them [juveniles] in first grade, if you don't get them in second grade, well if you get behind, you never seem to catch up. . . . We must lay a solid foundation. We must teach reading, writing and values. That is where the major focus must be.[2]

Recent studies show that our juvenile prisons in the United States are overcrowded and expose young people to the conditions of prison life that the juvenile justice system was supposed to prevent.

The statistics are piling up at an astounding rate. According to figures reported in *NJEA Review*, a teachers' magazine, the juvenile violent crime arrest rate increased by 19 percent for African Americans and by 44 percent for Caucasians between 1980 and 1990. Homicide, the report went on, is the third leading cause of death for children age ten to fourteen, and the second leading cause of death for youths between the ages of fifteen and twenty-four.[3]

Sometimes a program meets with unexpected success. Here is part of a speech given by a graduate from the Cape May County Sheriff's Department Youth Academy (boot camp) program in 1995:

> In the past 2 weeks at the Youth Academy we learned how to respect ourselves and others. In the beginning of the program it was real hard because we had to face 2 weeks without friends, family and officers telling us what to do all of the time. . . . The first thing we had

Between 1990 and 2010, the juvenile population in the U.S. will increase and become more racially and ethnically diverse

	Population		Increase	
	1990	2010	Number	%
All juveniles	64,185,000	73,617,000	9,432,000	15
Ages 0–4	18,874,000	20,017,000	1,143,000	6
Ages 5–9	18,064,000	19,722,000	1,658,000	9
Ages 10–14	17,191,000	20,724,000	3,533,000	21
Ages 15–17	10,056,000	13,154,000	3,098,000	31
White	51,336,000	55,280,000	3,944,000	8
Black	9,896,000	12,475,000	2,579,000	26
Native American	745,000	886,000	141,000	19
Asian/Pacific Islander	2,208,000	4,976,000	2,768,000	125
(Hispanic Origin*	7,886,000	13,543,000	5,657,000	71)

- Between 1990 and 2010, not only will the size of the juvenile population increase, but so will the average age.

- The growth in the white juvenile population between 1990 and 2010 will be the result of an increase in white-Hispanics; the number of non-Hispanic white juveniles is expected to decline over the period.

*Note: Race categories include persons of Hispanic origin. Persons of Hispanic origin can be of any race.

Sources: Bureau of the Census (1993). *Current population reports, U.S. population estimates by age, sex, race and Hispanic origin: 1980 to 1991.* Bureau of the Census. (1993). *Current population reports, population projections of the U.S., by age, sex, race and Hispanic origin: 1993 to 2050.*

The juvenile population of the United States has grown steadily in the past decade. Currently, 96 million Americans—more than one in four—are under the age of eighteen.

to do is accept the fact that we were here. A few people did not take this learning experience very well, therefore they did not do what they were told and most of all they did not respect other cadets or the officers, so they were dismissed from the program. . . . We are all proud of ourselves, we learned self discipline and respect along with other very important subjects. This program taught us how to deal with ourselves and others. No one can change if they don't want to and no one can change anyone else, but they can help others and themselves change. . . . We know there were times when we all wanted to give up, but we didn't. We stuck through it and made it as a team. Now we would like to express our class slogan: RESPECT—RESPONSIBILITY—ACCOUNTABILITY.

We need to create future generations of young people who respect themselves and each other. They must learn to accept the responsibility of caring for themselves and getting an education that will serve them in the future. Finally, young people must know in no uncertain terms that they will be held accountable for what they do. America is a country that was founded on laws to protect its citizens. People who break those laws must accept the punishment that goes with their actions. We owe it to ourselves, our families, and our communities to strive to continue to make the United States a safe and prosperous nation.

The Carnegie Council on Adolescent Development recently issued a report about America's teens. The report said that America is neglecting its ten- to fourteen-year-old children. This age group has become more at risk than any other and could become "lifelong casualties of substance abuse, AIDS, and other social ills."[4] The report placed blame for this problem on many issues, including single-parent families, declining parental interest in schools, and increased television watching. These are many of the same issues that have been presented as causes of the rapid rise of juvenile crime. Until many of these social issues are dealt with, reducing juvenile crime in America will continue to be difficult. It will be a job for all of us.

Chapter Notes

Chapter 1

1. Howard Snyder and Melissa Sickmund, *Juvenile Offenders and Victims: A Focus on Violence* (Washington, D.C.: Federal Bureau of Investigation, 1995), p. 11.

2. Michael Biskup, ed., *Youth Violence* (San Diego, Calif.: Greenhaven Press, 1992), p. 13.

3. Sara Glazer, "Violence in Schools," *CQ Researcher*, September 11, 1992, pp. 787–803.

4. Howard Snyder and Melissa Sickmund, *Juvenile Offenders and Victims: A National Report* (Washington, D.C.: Office of Juvenile Justice and Delinquency Prevention, 1995), pp. 47–51.

5. Ibid., pp. 101–102.

6. Biskup, p. 13.

7. Ralph Cipriano, "Save the Children," *Philadelphia Inquirer Magazine*, September 24, 1995, pp. 16–21.

8. Ted Gest and Dorian Friedman, "The New Crime Wave," *U.S. News and World Report*, August 29, 1994, p. 26.

9. Nancy R. Gibbs, "Murder in Miniature," *Time*, September 19, 1994, pp. 55–59.

10. Snyder and Sickmund, *Juvenile Offenders and Victims: A National Report*, p. 47.

11. R. Craig Sauter, "Standing Up to Violence," *Phi Delta Kappan*, vol. 76, no. 5, January 1995, p. K2.

Chapter 2

1. Elaine Landau, *Teens and the Death Penalty* (Hillside, N.J.: Enslow Publishers, Inc., 1992), pp. 66–69.

2. La Mar Empey, *Juvenile Justice: The Progressive Legacy and Current Reform* (Charlottesville, Va.: University of Virginia Press, 1979).

3. Clifford Simonsen, *Juvenile Justice in America* (Encino, Calif.: Glencoe Publishing Co., 1979), pp. 16–19.

4. Robert Drowns and Karen Hess, *Juvenile Justice* (St. Paul, Minn.: West Publishing Co., 1990), p. 9.

5. Ibid., pp. 297–298.

6. Barry Krisberg and James F. Austin, *Reinventing Juvenile Justice* (Newberry Park, Calif.: Sage Publishers, 1993), p. 21.

7. Ibid., p. 30.

8. Drowns and Hess, p. 13.

9. Mark Jacobs, *Screwing the System and Making It Work* (Chicago: University of Chicago Press, 1990), p. 6.

10. Ibid.

11. Ira Schwartz, *Justice for Juveniles* (Lexington, Mass.: Lexington Books, 1989), p. 4.

12. Daniel Katkin et. al., *Delinquency and the Juvenile Justice System* (North Scituate, Mass.: Duxbury Press, 1994).

13. Monrad Paulsen et. al., *Juvenile Law and Procedure* (Reno, Nev.: National Council of Juvenile Court Judges, 1974), p. 3.

14. *In re* Gault, 18LE 2d 527 (1967).

15. *Crime in the United States*, p. 81, as cited in Howard Snyder and Melissa Sickmund, *Juvenile Offenders and Victims: A National Report* (Washington, D.C.: Office of Juvenile Justice and Delinquency Prevention, 1995), p. 81.

Chapter 3

1. Dean E. Murphy, "The Rise in Kids Who Kill," *Los Angeles Times*, August 16, 1992, p. 1.

2. Ibid.

3. Tamara Chuang, "10 Charged as Police Take Aim at Gangs," *Philadelphia Inquirer*, August 19, 1995, p. B1.

4. Ibid.

5. "An Explosion of Juvenile Crime," *U.S. News and World Report*, March 25, 1996, p. 30.6. "Crack: A Cheap and Deadly Cocaine," *Time*, June 2, 1986, p. 18.

7. R. Barri Flowers, *The Adolescent Criminal* (Jefferson, N.C.: McFarland & Co., 1990), pp. 90–92.

8. *Youth and Alcohol: Selected Reports to the Surgeon General* (Washington, D.C.: U.S. Department of Education, 1994), p. 27.

9. Howard Snyder and Melissa Sickmund, *Juvenile Offenders and Victims: A National Report* (Washington, D.C.: Office of Juvenile Justice and Delinquency Prevention, 1995), p. 64.

10. Ibid.

11. Jim Impoco and Monika Guttman, "Hollywood: Right Face," *U.S. News and World Report*, May 15, 1995, pp. 66–72.

12. Ibid.

13. Holly Metz, "Kids in the Cuckoo's Nest," *Progressive*, December 1991, p. 26.

14. J. D. Halloran and R. L. Brown, *Television and Delinquency* (Leicester, U.K.: Leicester University Press, 1976), p. 9.

15. Nancy Wartik, "Why Some Kids Go Wrong," *McCalls*, April 1994, p. 100.

16. Richard Lacayo, "Violent Action," *Time*, June 12, 1995, pp. 24–30.

17. Snyder and Sickmund, p. 220.

Chapter 4

1. Ramsey Clark, *Crime in America* (New York: Pocket Books, 1971), p. 220.

2. Howard Snyder and Melissa Sickmund, *Juvenile Offenders and Victims: A National Report* (Washington, D.C.: Office of Juvenile Justice and Delinquency Prevention, 1995), p. 75.

3. *A Guide for Juvenile Conference Committees* (Trenton, N.J.: New Jersey Administrative Office of the Courts, January 1988), pp. 10–15.

4. Snyder and Sickmund, p. 141.

5. Barry Krisberg, *Reinventing Juvenile Justice* (Newbury Park, Calif.: Sage Publishers, 1993), p. 79.

6. Clifford Simonsen, *Juvenile Justice in America* (Encino, Calif: Glencoe Publishing Co., 1979), p. 161.

7. Ibid.

8. Irving Slott, "On the Front Lines: Interview with Judge David B. Mitchell," *Juvenile Justice*, Spring/Summer 1993, Vol. 1, No. 1, pp. 8–16.

9. Ibid.

10. Ibid.

11. Simonsen, pp. 193–203.

12. Robert Drowns and Karen Hess, *Juvenile Justice* (St. Paul, Minn.: West Publishing Co., 1990), p. 303.

13. Snyder and Sickmund, p. 165.

14. Simonsen, pp. 219–230.

15. Snyder and Sickmund, p. 154.

Chapter 5

1. Detective Michael Brogan, personal interview, July 21, 1995.

2. Lieutenant Daniel Placentra, personal interview, February 7, 1996.

3. Ibid.

4. Ibid.

5. Brogan, personal interview.

6. Ibid.

7. Ibid.

8. Ibid.

9. Ibid.

Chapter 6

1. Michael Biskup, ed., *Youth Violence* (San Diego, Calif.: Greenhaven Press, 1992), pp. 210–211.

2. Alex Kotlowitz, "Their Crimes Don't Make Them Adults," *The New York Times Magazine*, February 13, 1994, pp. 40–41.

3. *Juvenile Justice Bulletin*, October 1994, p. 1.

4. "Skinhead Pair Face Adult Trial in Family's Death," *Philadelphia Inquirer*, September 6, 1995, p. B3.

5. Howard Snyder and Melissa Sickmund, *Juvenile Offenders and Victims: A Focus on Violence* (Pittsburg, Pa.: National Center for Juvenile Justice, 1995), p. 30.

6. Biskup, pp. 210–211.

7. Ron Rosenbaum, "Too Young to Die?," *The New York Times Magazine*, March 12, 1989, pp. 32–35, 58–61.

8. Robert Drowns and Karen Hess, *Juvenile Justice* (St. Paul, Minn.: West Publishing Co., 1990), p. 246.

9. "Judgment Day," *People Weekly*, August 29, 1994, p. 90.

10. Charles Patrick Ewing, *Kids Who Kill* (New York: Avon Books, 1992), p. 228.

11. Laura Mansnerus, "Treating Teen-agers as Adults in Court," *The New York Times*, December 3, 1993, pp. 787–803.

12. Kotlowitz, p. 41.

Chapter 7

1. Jay Albanese, *Dealing With Delinquency* (Hyland, Md.: University Press of America, 1985), p. 105.

2. David Johnson and Roger Johnson, *Reducing School Violence Through Conflict Resolution* (Alexandria, Va.: Association for Curriculum and Development, 1995), pp. 20–22.

3. "Easing Violence With Student Help," *The New York Times*, December 26, 1993, p. 37.

4. "Teenage Defendants Get Juries of Their Peers," *Wall Street Journal*, June 3, 1994, p. B8.

5. Roberta Cronin, "Boot Camps for Adults and Juvenile Offenders," *National Institute of Justice Research Report*, October 1994, pp. 33–39.

6. "Sergeant Henry Johnson Youth Leadership Academy and City Challenger," *New York State Division for Youth Report*, June 1995, pp. 1–5.

7. Mark Cohen, "Uncle Milty's Lost Kids," *The New York Times Magazine*, August 1, 1993, pp. 30–34.

8. Dr. Jill A. Gordon, *Paint Creek Youth Center: A Program Description* (Ph.D. paper, University of Cincinnati), pp. 10–11.

9. Elizabeth Gleick, "The Call of the Wild," *Time*, June 26, 1995, p. 64.

10. Holly Metz, "Kids in the Cuckoo's Nest," *Progressive*, December 1991, pp. 22–25.

Chapter 8

1. Fox Butterfield, "Grim Forecast Is Offered on Rising Juvenile Crime," *The New York Times*, September 8, 1995, p. A16.

2. Speech by State Senator William Gormley, Ventnor City Hall, New Jersey, August 25, 1995.

3. George D. Comerci, "Preventing Violence," *NJEA Review*, October 1995, p. 10.

4. "Study Says Young Teens Are America's Most Neglected," *Philadelphia Inquirer*, October 11, 1995.

Glossary

accessory—A person who assists or contributes to committing a crime.

assault—Intentional forced injury to another person.

cross-examine—In a trial, to question the witness who has already testified so the witness's truthfulness or reliability can be determined.

delinquency—The act of breaking laws that are established for everyone.

discrimination—The failure to treat all people equally, or showing favoritism or dislike to a special group of people.

due process—The provision in our legal system to protect the rights of the individual.

felony—A serious crime that may be punishable by imprisonment or death.

homicide—The killing of a person by another.

incarceration—Confining a person to a prison or other institution by law.

juvenile—A young person at or below the age of juvenile court jurisdiction, which may be age fifteen, sixteen, or seventeen depending on the state. See chart on page 73.

misdemeanor—A crime that is less serious than a felony, and is usually punishable by a fine or a short time in jail.

testify—Giving evidence or statements in court under oath.

vagrancy—The act of going from place to place without a home or any money.

waive—The process by which a juvenile court judge transfers a case to the adult court.

Further Reading

Books

Albanese, Jay. *Dealing with Delinquency.* Hyland, Md.: University Press of America, 1985.

Biskup, Michael, ed. *Youth Violence.* San Diego, Calif.: Greenhaven Press, 1992.

Clark, Ramsey. *Crime in America.* New York: Pocketbook Press, 1971.

Drowns, Robert W., and Karen Hess. *Juvenile Justice.* St. Paul, Minn.: West Publishing. Co., 1990.

Empey, La Mar T. *Juvenile Justice: The Progressive Legacy and Current Reform.* Charlottesville, Va.: University of Virginia Press, 1979.

Flowers, R. Barri. *The Adolescent Criminal.* Jefferson, N.C.: McFarland and Co., 1990.

Halloran, J.D., and R.L. Brown. *Television and Delinquency.* Leicester, U.K.: Leicester University Press, 1976.

Jacobs, Mark D. *Screwing the System and Making It Work.* Chicago: University of Chicago Press, 1990.

Jasper, Margaret. *Juvenile Justice and Children's Law.* Dobbs Ferry, N.Y.: Oceana Publishers, 1994.

Johnson, David W., and Roger T. Johnson. *Reducing School Violence.* Alexandria, Va.: ASCD Press, 1995.

Krisberg, Barry, and James F. Austin. *Reinventing Juvenile Justice.* Newberry Park, Calif.: Sage Publications, 1993.

Landau, Elaine. *Teens and the Death Penalty.* Hillside, N.J.: Enslow Publishers, Inc., 1992.

Paulsen, Monrad G., and Charles Whitebread. *Juvenile Law and Procedure.* Reno, Nev.: National Council of Juvenile Court Judges, 1974.

Schwartz, Ira M. *Justice for Juveniles.* Lexington, Mass.: Lexington Books, 1989.

Simonsen, Clifford, and Gordon Marshall III. *Juvenile Justice in America.* Encino, Calif.: Glencoe Publishing Co., 1979.

Snyder, Howard N., and Melissa Sickmund. *Juvenile Offenders and Victims: A National Report.* Washington, D.C.: Office of Juvenile Justice and Delinquency Prevention, 1995.

Youth and Alcohol: Selected Reports to the Surgeon General. Washington, D.C.: U.S. Department of Education, 1994.

Periodicals

Butterfield, Fox. "Grim Forecast is Offered on Rising Juvenile Crime." *The New York Times*, September 8, 1995.

Chuang, Tamara. "10 Charged as Police Take Aim at Gangs." *Philadelphia Inquirer*, August 19, 1995, B1.

Cipriano, Ralph. "Save the Children." *Philadelphia Inquirer Magazine*, September 24, 1995, 16–21.

Cohen, Mark. "Uncle Milty's Lost Kids." *The New York Times Magazine*, August 1, 1993, 30–34.

Comerci, George D. "Preventing Violence." *NJEA Review*, October 1995, 10–15.

"Crack: A Cheap and Deadly Cocaine." *Time*, June 2, 1986, 18.

Cronin, Roberta. "Boot Camps for Adults and Juvenile Offenders." *National Institute of Justice Research Report*, October 1994, 33–39.

"Easing Violence, with Students' Help." *The New York Times*, December 26, 1993, 37.

Gest, Ted, and Dorian Friedman. "The New Crime Wave." *U.S. News and World Report*, August 29, 1994, 26.

Gibbs, Nancy R. "Murder in Miniature." *Time*, September 19, 1994, 53–54.

Glazer, Sarah. "Violence in Schools." *CQ Researcher*, September 11, 1992, 787–803.

Gleick, Elizabeth. "The Call of the Wild." *Time*, June 26, 1995, 64.

"How Juveniles Get to Criminal Court." *Juvenile Justice Bulletin*, OJJDP, October 1994, 1–3.

"Judgment Day." *People Weekly*, August 29, 1994, 90.

Kotlowitz, Alex. "Their Crimes Don't Make Them Adults." *The New York Times Magazine*, February 13, 1994, 40–41.

Further Reading

Lacayo, Richard. "Violent Action." *Time*, June 12, 1995, 24–30.

Mansnerus, Laura. "Treating Teen Agers as Adults." *The New York Times*, December 3, 1993.

Metz, Holly. "Kids in the Cuckoo's Nest." *Progressive*, December 1991, 22–25.

National Institute for Justice Update, October 1994, 1.

"On the Front Lines: Interview with Judge David B. Mitchell." *Juvenile Justice,* Vol. 1, No. 1, Spring/Summer 1993, 8–16.

Pipho, Chris. "States Get Tough on Juvenile Crime." *Phi Delta Kappan*, December 1993, 286–287.

Rosenbaum, Ron. "Too Young to Die?" *The New York Times Magazine*, March 12, 1989.

Sauter, R. Craig. "Standing Up to Violence." *Phi Delta Kappan*, Vol. 65, No. 5, January 1995, K1–K12.

Wartik, Nancy. "Why Some Kids Go Wrong." *McCalls*, April 1994, 94ff.

Index

A
adjudication process, 46
alcohol and teens, 32, 34

B
boot camp, 83–86
Bridewell's, 52
Brogan, Mike, 56, 59–60, 61, 62–63

C
Carnegie Council on Adolescent Development, 97–98
Child Savers, 20
Children's Aid Society, 20
correction facilities, 51
custody, 41

D
D.A.R.E. (Drug Awareness Resistance Education), 89–91, 93
detention centers, 45–46
division programs, 41
drugs and teens, 32–34, 35

F
FBI Crime Data, 6, 37

G
gangs, 30–31, 57, 60
Gault, Jerry, 25–27
Gormley, William, 94–95
G.R.E.A.T. (Gang Resistance Education and Training), 91, 93
guns, 31–32

H
Houses of Refuge, 17–18

J
juvenile arrest rate, 13
Juvenile Conference Committee, 41–43, 66
juvenile court, 46, 48–50
Juvenile Delinquency and Prevention Act, 21
juvenile intake, 44
Juvenile Justice and Delinquency Prevention Act, 21, 23
juveniles in adult court, 67–68

K
Kent, Morris, 24-25

L
Lower Township police, 62–63

M
media, 35–36
mental hospitals, 88–89
Milton Hershey School, 86, 87
Miranda warnings, 63

N
New York City, 7, 18, 30
North Star Expeditions, 92

O
Ocuish, Hannah, 16

P
Paint Creek Youth Center, 87–88, 93
parole, 53–54
peer mediation, 79–81
Philadelphia, 9
Placentra, Dan, 56–59, 60
probation, 24, 50–51

R
reform schools, 18

S
Sandifer, Robert "Yummy," 12–14
Scared Straight Program, 78–79
Supreme Court decisions
  Kent v. *United States*, 24–25
  In Re *Gault*, 25–27, 66
  Mckeiver v. *Pennsylvania*, 76

T
Teen Court, 81, 83

U
United States Children's Bureau, 21

W
White Conference on Youth, 21

Y
Youth Leadership Academy, 84–86
Youth Offenses Act, 21